INTRODUCTION

With 281,000 units produced, the High Mobility Multipurpose Wheeled Vehicle (HMMWV), or Humvee, has rapidly earned its place in pop culture as the all-round action vehicle of the late twentieth century. Endorsed by actor Arnold Schwarzenegger, the Humvee became the face of a revitalized post-Vietnam US military.

The Humvee was the result of a decade-long search to find the perfect military vehicle. Saddled with an ageing utility vehicle fleet, patched together with off-the-shelf civilian offerings, the US military was in need of something universally dynamic. Design teams were faced with the task of merging the best aspects of five in-service vehicles, and drawing inspiration from the original utility truck, the Jeep, to provide a worthy replacement.

The 1970s and 1980s saw the US military looking at new ways of working to become logistically, tactically and strategically sleeker and more flexible. With the inauguration of Ronald Reagan and his unifying campaign slogan 'Let's Make America Great Again', the timing of the new project couldn't have been better. Reagan was determined to rebuild American industrial and military prestige, especially after the late 1970s oil crisis had nearly destroyed that cornerstone of the American Dream, the automobile industry.

With an almost immediate rise in defence spending, the US was able to consolidate and concentrate on developing a universal force. This would centre on the newly introduced M1 Abrams Main Battle Tank, and M2 Bradley Infantry Fighting Vehicle, supplemented by M113s and the new Humvee. The days of a streamlined, easily deployable force were upon the US military.

By 1985 the first of AM General's new Humvees were in service, and within 15 years a mind-boggling range of variants would be available in service with over 50 countries. Air portable, rugged and adaptable, the Humvee was everything the US wanted and more. With impressive cross-country performance, stability and, most importantly of all, aggressive looking, the clean-lined Humvee was a hit.

First seen in Operation Just Cause in 1989, it certainly raised eyebrows, with commentators and enthusiasts in awe as Humvees raced to secure areas, or were

A crew cab M998 equipped with a small shelter ready for patrol. Note the bed rolls and field packs attached to the sides. (SSG Arnold Kalmanson)

M998 of the 7th Light Infantry Division disembarks from a C-5 Galaxy. Note the M105 trailer. (A1C Scott R. Gibson)

A fine study of an early display during the army logistics exposition PROLOG'85. (SSG Arnold W. Kalmanson)

A convoy prepares to move out during Operation Desert Storm. The M998 in the foreground tows the awesome M167 20mm Vulcan anti-aircraft gun. (SPC Elliott)

A well-placed M998 in front of an M60 Armoured Vehicle Launched Bridge (AVLB) at a forward USMC camp in northern Saudi Arabia during Operation Desert Shield. (CW2 Ed Bailey)

used as improvised checkpoints. From then on, the Humvee was ever present and within a year it would once again find itself in action, this time patrolling the deserts of South West Asia.

As the Cold War ended and international borders shifted, the work of the United Nations, and in time NATO, became ever more important. Peacekeeping missions developed into implementation, stability and intervention forces. In these roles the Humvee had the edge, especially in areas where roads were almost non-existent or in a poor state of repair. However, the threats that these new missions brought meant that the Humvee needed to be strengthened and so the Humvee became an armoured platform, capable of protecting troops from mine blasts and small-arms fire.

As its influence grew the Humvee became an export success, and was even reverse-engineered by Chinese as the EQ2050. By the turn of the century, AM General were able to field 15 official variants and dozens more 'unofficial' types. Whilst a replacement programme with the Joint Light Tactical Vehicle (JLTV) is underway, the Humvee is set to remain in service until at least 2050.

For the modeller the Humvee represents a fount of inspiration and opportunity, as well as the possibility of producing some wonderful camouflage finishes. From UN peacekeeping missions to dioramas based in Central Europe to action-packed desert vignettes, the Humvee really is a great foundation for some creative modelling ideas.

Design & Development

Left: A night live-fire training exercise lights up an up-armoured M1114 of 490th Civil Affairs Battalion (CAB), 155th Brigade Combat Team (BCT), at the Iraqi Army compound firing range on Forward Operating Base (FOB) Iskandariyah, Iraq. (PFC Edward G. Martens, USN)

Below: Vintage Jeeps line the streets of Sainte-Mère-Église, France, to commemorate the 60th anniversary of D-Day. (A1C Steven Czyz, USAF)

Beginnings and Briefs

The late 1970s' US army motor pool held some 600,000 tactical vehicles including the original Jeep replacement and not always stable M151 MUTT. Also fielded were the M561 Gama Goat, the M274 Mule and the 1¼-ton Kaiser Jeep M715. On top of this were nearly 45,000 M880 light utility vehicles – or Commercial Utility Cargo Vehicles (CUCVs). These were militarized Dodge 4x4 and 4x2 (M890) pickup trucks which fulfilled general non-tactical roles from ambulances to maintenance vehicles.

Despite having a huge number of vehicles, partially as a result of the Vietnam War, this pool did not always equate to roadworthy assets. Indeed, it was recommended that of the 600,000 vehicles, two-thirds needed replacement. On the face of it this was a staggering number: the timing, financially and politically, was wrong and the US military was suffering a post-Vietnam crisis of confidence.

In 1977 President Carter, faced with growing Soviet military confidence and influence, increased military spending. Not only would this help develop new ideas, but also increase US commercial influence in the world market. The timing could not have been better as the US was able to begin planning a programme of vehicle rationalization whilst preparing for the introduction of third-generation tracked and wheeled assets. Added to this was the knowledge that the power of the BGM-71 TOW anti-tank, anti-bunker missile system

Marines secure canvas covers on M40 106mm recoilless rifles using M274 utility platform trucks as portees somewhere in Vietnam. (PFC Kenneth L. Fuller)

Right: Two M792 Gama Goat ambulances parked near a detention compound for Cuban nationals captured during Operation Urgent Fury, the invasion of Grenada. (Combined Military Service Digital Photographic Files)

Below: An M880 tests water resistance and salt-water corrosion protection during the fording phase of the research for the Grease, Automotive and Artillery Candidates Test at the Army Tropic Test Center. (Combined Military Service Digital Photographic Files)

had been underestimated, especially in the portee role. Sadly, the unstable M151 was not deemed suitable so a new vehicle was sought.

US Army Tank/Automotive & Armaments Command (TACOM) looked to develop an everyman approach with the new light utility truck. The name of the new project to meet these demands was the XM966 Combat Support Vehicle (CSV) Program. Four manufacturers, keen to fill production and financial gaps left by declining automotive sales, stepped up to the challenge: Chrysler, Cadillac-Gage, Teledyne Continental and AM General.

Prototypes were soon produced, yet nothing stood out for TACOM; however, the programme had sparked interest in the concept and by 1979 TACOM started a new programme: the HMMWV, soon to be known as the Humvee. The HMMWV or High Mobility Multipurpose Wheeled Vehicle, aimed to deliver 50,000 tactical vehicles to replace all ¼-ton to 1¼-ton vehicles, whilst covering Army, Marine and Air Force needs. Planned to have a 1¼-ton capacity and be totally adaptable to for a range of tasks, as well as being air-transportable, it was envisaged the Humvee would spend 40 per cent of its time off-road, 30 per cent on highways and 30 per cent on minor roads.

TACOM released the four key objectives for the HMMWV, to:

- provide a single vehicle family to satisfy joint service requirements.
- provide a vehicle with excellent cross-country and on-road performance.
- provide a replacement vehicle for the M274 Mule, M561 Gama Goat and M792 Ambulance.
- selectively replace the M151 Jeep and M880 Truck.

The idea was refined and submitted to Congress for consideration and a letter of interest was sent to Chrysler Defence, AM General and Teledyne to develop the idea.

The Design Process

From the outset it was envisaged that the Humvee would need to be both a light and sturdy utility vehicle. To that end a new way of thinking was encouraged and so the Humvee would be a general-purpose tactical utility vehicle. It would also be a prime mover, a specialized equipment carrier, a weapons carrier and an ambulance. To bring the new vehicle in line with changing NATO fuel standards, it would also be diesel powered.

Chrysler Defence was the first concern to drop out of the 'competition' after being purchased by General Dynamics Land Systems (GDLS) in spring 1982, leaving AM General, who had opted to fit full-time 4x4 to their prototype, and Teledyne to compete. AM General's involvement was driven by pride as much as it was by commercial interest. As the owners of the Kaiser Jeep brand they were keen to wrestle the laurels back from Ford's M151 MUTT.

AM General had also been developing a tactical truck, privately, since 1979, which they had branded as the 'Hummer', in the hope it would repeat the commercial

Design & Development

Left: The rear-engined, petrol-powered XR311 was a useful exercise for AM General in more ways than one.

Below: Members of the 2nd Battalion, 80th Division (Institutional Training (IT)) fire a Mk 19 40mm grenade launcher, MOD 3, from an M1025. (Keith Dillon)

successes of the Jeep. This tactical truck had its roots in a private venture of Food Machinery Corps (FMC), a noted military vehicle producer, as the XR311. Whilst trialled in the late 1960s and early 1970s and doing well, the XR311 failed to take off for financial reasons. As FMC wanted to concentrate on their tracked vehicle lines, they sold the rights to AM General. However, the XR311 had a rear-mounted engine so adjustments were necessary to ensure it fitted TACOM's exacting brief.

AM General weren't the only company with a head start. In 1977 Teledyne became involved in the Combat Support Vehicle (CSV) programme with their XM966 Cheetah. The Cheetah had a lightweight aluminium and fibreglass body and like the XR311 mounted a rear engine. The CSV programme would be sidelined by the HMMWV Program, but like AM General it gave Teledyne a head start.

For the HMMWV Program AM General set out to build the definitive military utility truck: utilitarian, flexible, tough and reliable. It was based on a common diesel engine mounted into a sturdy chassis which also housed the power train. The Humvee would utilize interchangeable parts to produce 15 different vehicle configurations.

The chassis is a tapered steel box-section ladder type, featuring five cross-members, with a noticeable drop in its longitudinal beams. The engine (positioned at a slight angle), gearbox, drive train and fuel tanks all sitting between the beams. The rear bumper and towing pintle are attached to the rear cross-member while prominent lifting eyes protrude from the bonnet.

The original engine was a General Motors V8 6.1l diesel which produced 130bhp at 3,600rpm, and was already in use with the CUCV range, keeping spares costs low. The cooling system is a liquid-based type, and to ensure the bonnet height was kept as low as possible, the radiator lies over the front portion of the engine. Transmission is an engine-mounted General Motors THM400HD Hydramatic three-speed automatic transmission (3F1R). The transfer box is a New Process NP218 full-time four-wheel drive unit. For suspension AM General elected to fit double A-frame and coils to front and rear, using as many identical elements as possible to ensure ease of maintenance and keep costs low.

Whilst of a later M1100 series Humvee, the chassis arrangement remains the same. Note the slightly off-centre engine and forward sling hooks either side of the radiator.

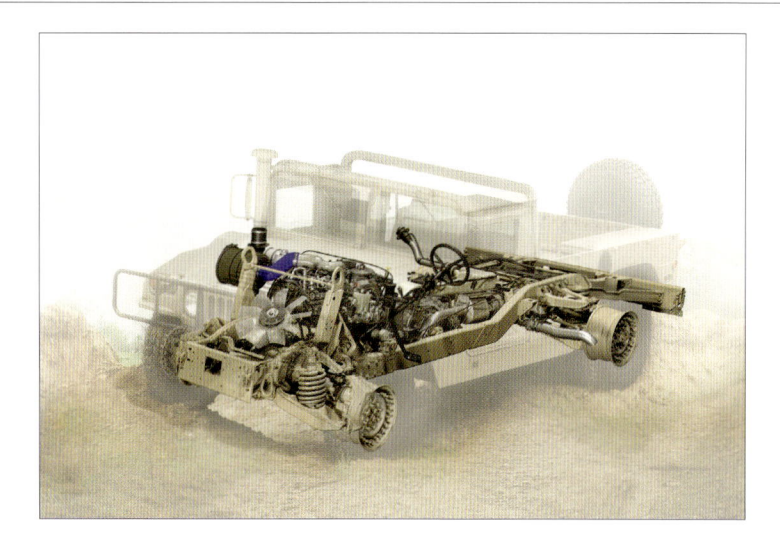

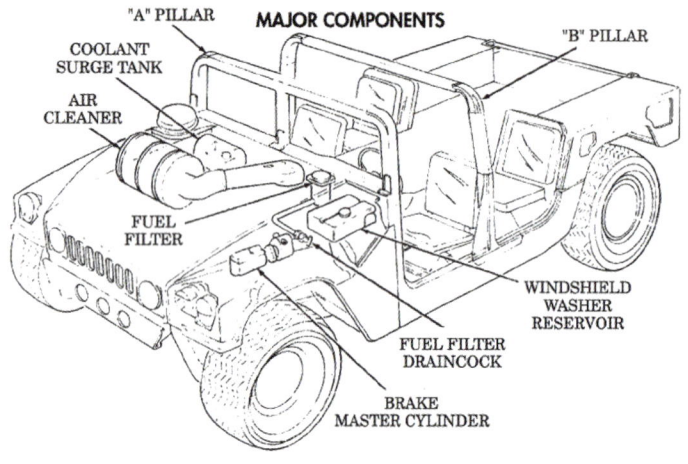

This wonderful cutaway image shows how all the mechanical elements of the Humvee come into play. (AM General)

Underside of an upside-down M998. Note engine and power train elements. (LCPL Alvarado)

The bodywork consisted of an aluminium frame formed as a type of tub, to which the body panels are either riveted or epoxy fixed. The body panels are constructed from 6010-grade heat-treatable magnesium-silicon aluminium alloy which was chosen for its light weight and corrosion-resistant properties. The unique bonnet is a semi-moulded plastic laminate which features another identifying feature of the Humvee, the upper bonnet louvres for the radiator. These are internally baffled to prevent debris damage to the face of the radiator underneath.

The body sits either side of the chassis which keeps the silhouette low, making it 1.87m at the top of the 'A' pillar; it also keeps the centre of gravity low, which aids for easy handling, especially at speed. The tub features a raised centre section to allow for engine and transmission clearance. This feature allows for the mounting of the Single Channel Ground and Airborne Radio System (SINCGARS) radio set as well as a standing platform for the gunner in the armament carrier versions.

Steering is power assisted using a Saginaw 708 variable ratio integral unit which gives the Humvee a turning circle of 7.6m (25ft). Brakes are hydraulically operated inboard discs whilst the tyres were fitted to split-rim 16.5in rims, held together by eight nuts, which changed to 12 on later models and 24 on M1100 series Humvees. The wheels were fitted with magnesium run-flat inserts that allowed the vehicle to travel up to 30mph on one flat tyre and 20mph on two. To prevent any potentially reputation-damaging mistakes AM General put the Humvee through an exacting 17,000 miles on their own track before being releasing it to TACOM's demanding testing teams.

Proofing the Design
The prototype trials started in the summer of 1982 at Maryland's Aberdeen Proving Ground (APG), and the vast Yuma Proving Ground (YPG) of Arizona where the desert environment would provide a suitable challenge. As with all tests a series of minor engineering issues were raised, which once corrected saw the second phase of testing at Fort Hunter-Liggett in California, completed by serving personnel. By the end of 1982 the third phase of testing started, which applied real-time scenarios that the military user might encounter, including navigating challenging terrain and crossing water obstacles. Throughout the trials AM General's Humvee was the clear winner as a result of the soundness of its design and development.

As with all things new there were issues. The General Motors DDA V8 diesel, for example, was a commercial unit, and gave slight cause for concern with its seemingly random failures. Ultimately this was changed for a GM Detroit-Diesel Allison 6.2l V8 capable of producing 150bhp at 2,000rpm. The electrical system also suffered a few hiccups, involving the vital lighting sets. The issue was eventually narrowed down to the excess vibration which was alleviated by relocating the lights and strengthening the connections. The cross-country tests highlighted the need for strengthening to be made to the door hinges of the armament carrier, while the aluminium used to construct the hub and suspension arm castings was substituted for stronger cast iron. Water-crossing activities also showed that there had been some liquid ingress into both drive train and instruments. This particular situation was easily addressed with the addition of new seals.

One final change was to the front grille. Feeling confident, AM General designers went for broke and remodelled the front grilles. Now, rather than being horizontal openings, they had morphed into vertical ones, similar to those found on the iconic Jeep. These changes and soundness of the original design must have been successful as AM General excelled. On 22 March 1983 AM General received a contract for 2,334 M998s, each costing $20,410. This was the first order of a $1.2 billion five-year-long contract in which 55,000 Humvees would be supplied.

In 1984 12 preproduction Humvees were sent to both APG and YPG for 'initial production testing'. To ensure the Humvee's suitability as a military asset, this phase of testing would include basic tyre changing to vigorous cross-country driving at speed. The latter revealed issues with the propeller shaft, which would break when the vehicle was driven above 70mph. After further testing AM General engineers identified the issue was due to harmonic vibration. A simple solution was found: limit the speed to 65mph and replace the propeller shaft with a two-piece item and a centre-bearing race. The upgraded vehicles drove over 15,000 miles (23,300km) without further incident.

The second phase test took place at Fort Hunter-Liggett, where five new preproduction vehicles were driven 5,000 miles (8,050km) over a six-week period. The next tests saw two vehicles go to Camp Pendleton and Coronado Amphibious Base where 1,200 miles (1,930km) of beach testing was undertaken. The remaining three were sent to Kentucky's Fort Knox where the Humvees covered 3,000 miles

PO Ben Nelson replaces rear suspension components at Forward Operating Base Apache, Zabul Province, Afghanistan. Note the brake disc to Nelson's right. (Mass Communication Specialist 1st Class David M. Votroubek)

Senior Airman (SRA) Aaron Hatfield, a vehicle maintenance journeyman, replaces the alternator at a Forward Deployed Location (FDL) in support of Operation Enduring Freedom. Note slight angle of windscreen. (SSG William Greer, USAF)

An M1097 showing off its Jeepesque grille, belonging to the Tactical Imagery Production System (TIPS) of 1st Marine Division (MD), Division Main's (DM's) Combat Camera and Printing Section halts in Basra Province, Southern Iraq during Operation Iraqi Freedom. (MSG Howard J. Farrell, USMC)

(4,828km) in a temperate environment, similar to Northern Europe's. This phase of testing was completed at YPG with vehicles covering 20,000 miles (32,186km) and two covering a further 40,000 miles (64374km). One interesting test was that of a solitary M988 sent to Alaska in March 1985 for cold-weather testing. There it covered 10,000 miles (16,100km) in temperatures as low as -45°C (-50°F) at Fort Greely, the Cold Region Test Center.

The tests highlighted some changes were needed, and these produced vehicles that were an improvement on the initial production batch produced by AM General's Mishawaka plant in January 1985. The key changes were the axle and torque converter ratios, redesigns of drive train, modifications of the power train and relocation of the engine and radiator units. A shortening of the chassis was also needed.

The Humvee Family of Vehicles
The Humvees were produced in five distinct categories which had been tested as prototypes during the development phase: the basic carrier, the armament carrier, the TOW carrier, the shelter carrier and finally the ambulance. Production of the first 54,973 Humvees started in April 1984 at AM General's Mishawaka plant in Indiana. This 96-acre site features the Military Assembly Plant (MAP) and the Flexible Assembly & Manufacturing Facility (FAMC), alongside a purpose-built one-mile-long test track. The first production vehicles began to roll off the assembly line on 4 January 1985, before being sent for testing to ensure they met contractual requirements. Once final testing had been completed, the first batches were released for service in October 1985.

Humvees were split into two distinct groups: Group I Humvees fulfilled essentially frontline and direct support roles. These included the M998 and M1038 Troop and Cargo Carriers, the M996 TOW Carrier, the M1025 and M1026 Armament Carriers; Group II vehicles comprised the command and control type and featured the M1037 and M1042 Shelter Carriers and the M997 and M1035 Ambulances. Base model vehicles can climb 60 per cent slopes and traverse a side slope of up to 40 per cent whilst fully loaded. The maximum fording depth, without the deep-water fording kit, is 0.76m (30in) and 1.52cm (60in) with the kit.

The M998 and M1038 Troop versions, including A1 and A2, form the base cargo and troop carrier models of the Humvee family of vehicles (FOV), capable of transporting a crew of two with a load of 1,135kg (2,500lb). As a troop carrier it is able to transport passengers using the troop seat kit, which features simple wooden slat benches that sit atop the squared wheel arches either side of the cargo bed. Another version features a four-person crew cab. Each version's crew area could be covered with a woven plastic tilt which left the cargo bed exposed to the elements, though this could be covered with a separate tilt.

The M1038 is equipped with a Warn Severe Duty 24v 12,000lb self-recovery winch to help self-extract from difficult

Above: A test USMC M1025 is equipped with four separate tracks during 34 days at the Mountain Warfare Training Center, California, for cold weather and arctic warfare training. (LCPL. E. J. Young)

Right: Mexican Army M998 on 16 September 2007 parade. (Carlos Valenzuela)

terrain. Like the M998 it can also operate as a troop carrier and is capable of transporting eight personnel.

The M966 Ambulance and the M1045 and M1167 TOW anti-tank missile carrier versions, including the A1 and A2 versions, are fitted with additional armour. Like the armament carrier the TOW carrier features the sloped rear, designed to prevent blast damage by a launched missile. The TOW launcher can be traversed through 360 degrees, depressed 10 degrees and elevated to 20 degrees. A 7.62mm general-purpose machine gun can be installed on the port side of the launcher for self-protection, and the M1167 features an enhanced protection basket for the gunner. Capable of carrying six missiles in the cargo compartment, the TOW Humvee offers a flexible and cost-effective field-based anti-tank capability. All versions have identical cross-country and fording capabilities as the M998, with the M1036, M1046 and M1167 fitted with the Warn Severe Duty winch.

The M1025 and M1026, including the A1 and A2 versions, alongside the up-armoured M1043 and M1044 versions, are the base armament carrier versions of the Humvee. All are fitted with a universal mount fixed to small roof-mounted turret ring which can be traversed through 360 degrees. This mount is capable of carrying the standard M60 7.62mm general-purpose machine gun, the potent M2 .50-cal machine gun and the Mk 19 40mm belt-fed automatic grenade launcher. These Humvees are used for force protection and projection roles. All versions have the same cross-country and fording capabilities as the M998, with the M1026 and M1044 fitted with the Warn Severe Duty winch.

The M1025 and M1026 and the M1035 Ambulance are fitted with a very basic armour, which consists of steel, Kevlar and varying thicknesses of polycarbonate windows to provide protection. This armour gives the occupants protection against spent bullets and shell fragments, provided they are travelling slower than 425m/s.

The M1037 and M1042, including the A1 and A2 versions, are the shelter carrier versions used to secure and transport a range of shelter types with a total payload, including the two crew, of 1,633kg (3,600lb). Both versions have the same cross-country and fording capabilities as the M998 with the M1042 fitted with the Warn Severe Duty winch.

There are four main all-weather general-purpose shelters available for use with the shelter carrier. Three utilize the same polyurethane foam core and aluminium skins sandwich for their construction. All can be carried by air assets and are available in either shielded or unshielded guises. The GSS-1497 Lightweight Shelter is an electronic equipment shelter fitted with a framework of high-strength welded and riveted aluminium alloy extrusions for mounting equipment. Due to the GSS-1497's size, there is a considerable rear overhang. The S-250 shelter is slightly smaller, sitting comfortably in the cargo area of the carrier. The S-710 Military Shelter is the largest of the shelters available, and when fitted gives the shelter carrier the appearance of a Luton-bodied box van.

The Standardized Integrated Command Post System (SICPS) Rigid Wall Shelter (RWS) S-787 is a self-contained unit constructed from a sandwich of aluminium and honeycomb-core. It features a 10kW generator, and is equipped with all fixtures necessary for the operation of the Army Tactical Command, Control and Communications System (ATC3S). An 11ft x 11ft Modular Command Post System Tent (MCPS), which is carried in an accompanying trailer, can be fitted to the rear of the S-787.

A US Marine from 2nd Battalion, 3rd Marines, mans a TOW missile launcher during a live-fire exercise at Pohakuloa training area on the Big Island of Hawaii: a fine study of the launch station in transit. (LCPL Simon Martin, USMC)

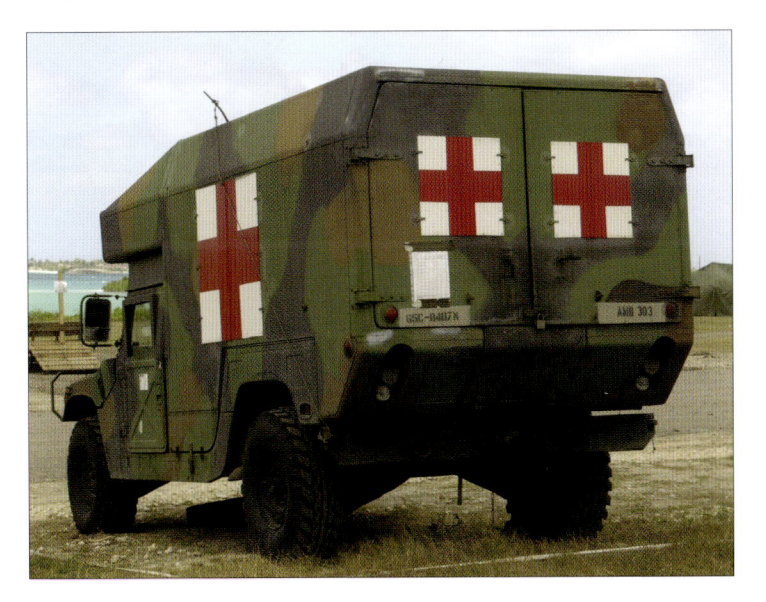

An M997 Ambulance from the 369th Combat Support Hospital (CSH), Puerto Rico, sits on the Crabbs Peninsula, Antigua, during the Tradewinds 2002 Field Training Exercise (FTX). Note the small door to the left of the steps, which is used to store stretchers. (Michelle A. Sosa)

A column of M1037s with S-250 shelter carriers and generator trailers waits near the T-AKR 302 USNS *William W. Seay*, at the Military Sealift Command (MSC), Port of Savannah. (Don Teft)

The final shelter is the S-788, constructed as per the S-787, and is designed to support Command, Control, Communications and Intelligence (C3I) missions and is available in three variants: Type 1 is the basic shelter, Type 2 is equipped with generator, escape hatch and chemical and biological (CB) purge valve, and Type 3 is equipped with just the generator.

The ambulance versions, the M997 and M1035, including the A1, A2 and A3 (M997 only) versions, are used to transport casualties safely from the front line to field hospitals. The M997 is able to transport four stretcher cases, eight walking wounded or a combination of both while the M1035 is a smaller soft-top version capable of transporting up to two stretcher cases, six walking wounded or a combination of both. The construction of hardtop versions is a sandwich of 25mm (1in) polyurethane foam covered externally with thin aluminium alloy. The walls and roof are further lined with Kevlar to provide ballistic protection for the occupants.

As well as carrying a full range of medical equipment required for treating trauma injuries, the M997 can be heated, ventilated or air-conditioned. For operation in a nuclear, biological or chemical (NBC) environment, the M977 is equipped with a Gas-Particulate Filter Unit (GPFU) with heaters. This system is capable of providing filtered air to up to seven personnel wearing either M25-series protective masks or M13-series patient-protective masks. Access to temperature-controlled and filtered air makes breathing easier whilst reducing the stress and heat fatigue that are often encountered when operating for extended periods in an NBC environment. Both versions have the same cross-country and fording capabilities as the M998, while the Warn Severe Duty winch is only fitted to the M1035A2 version.

The US Marine Corps (USMC) have their own unique requirements for their Humvees: these include removing the rear bumper to allow for easy egress from landing craft ramps, additional armour and special

A USMC M997 Ambulance stands by as the USMC UH-60 Black Hawk takes off to medevac (medical evacuation) an injured Marine outside of Camp Ripper, Kuwait. (LCPL Kevin C. Quihuis Jr, USMC)

Marines installing antennas on a communications shelter after coming ashore at Blue Beach in their M1037 during Exercise Valiant Usher. Note snorkel and raised exhaust. (SGT Carter)

deep wading kits. The additional armour and reinforced windows and doors protect occupants against spent bullets and shell fragments, provided they are travelling slower than 650m/s. The USMC were unique in having three distinct variants of the Humvee in service: the M1043 and winch-equipped M1044 Armament Carrier, the M1045 and winch-equipped M1046 TOW Carrier and the M1035 soft-top two-litter ambulance.

Radio Fit

Many Humvees are fitted with the very high frequency-frequency modulation (VHF-FM) Single Channel Ground and Airborne Radio System (SINCGARS). SINCGARS is a Combat Net Radio (CNR) which is used by US and allied military forces designed around three systems: SINCGARS, the high-frequency (HF) radio and the SC tactical satellite (TACSAT). Each of these systems has differing capabilities and transmission characteristics, giving users a full suite of communication capabilities. As a part of the CNR network, the SINCGARS' primary role is voice transmission for command and control and it can transmit and receive from both surface and airborne users. SINCGARS can also transmit and receive secure data and facsimile transmissions through simple connections to relevant equipment.

Upgrading the Humvee: The A1/A2 Versions

The first key changes occurred in 1991 and were as a result of amendments to the Joint Mission Element Needs Statement (JMENS). This document laid out the qualities required for a Heavy Humvee Variant (HHV). Whilst not onerous, they were explicit and included the provision of an 'Arctic Kit', individual weapon mounts, an increased payload of up to 2,045kg (4,508lb) and the installation of a 200Ah generator. The most important changes were to the suspension, which was treated to a full upgrade to cope with the increased weight and expected towing duties. New rear springs, spring seat shocks and control arms were added, along with heavy-duty tyres and rims; meanwhile, the chassis was upgraded with new cross-members.

These changes would form the M1097 Prime Mover which would replace the M1069s that had previously fulfilled the role with more than a few issues, including imbalance as a result of the gun's weight bearing down on the towing eye. The M1097 is capable of transporting a payload including a crew of two, of 2,075kg (4,575lb). It is capable of powering external equipment and stores via a 200amp power cable and is fitted with stowage for ammunition and equipment. To accommodate its increased payload capacity, the M1097 is fitted with reinforced frame and cross-members, and lifting shackles. The suspension features heavy-duty rear springs and shock absorbers alongside reinforced control arms. The drive train features a modified transfer case and differential with adapted

Of great use to the modeller, a wonderful late-twentieth-century study of the Humvee's 'office' shows the SINCGARS in all its glory. (CW4 Mark D. Houdlette)

A USMC communications M1097 drives past a Landing Craft, Air Cushioned (LCAC) landing on Red Beach for an amphibious assault on Camp Pendleton, during Exercise Kernel Blitz. (JO2 (SW/AW) Tyler A. Swartz, USN)

gear ratios, with heavy-duty tyres and rims fitted as standard. The M1097 also replaces the M1037 and M1042 as a troop and cargo and shelter carrier.

The A1 series of upgrades started to roll off the production lines in 1994. These new Humvees would be fitted with the M1097's stronger suspension and chassis modifications along with improved half shafts, a new transfer case, a redesigned front axle assembly and new glow plugs. The last was welcomed by mechanics in particular, as the rear portion of the engine was tucked underneath the vehicle body. This meant that changing glow plugs, which had a habit of fusing themselves to the engine, far easier.

One major complaint had been the crew seats, especially the driver's, who often brought their own cushions with them to take the edge off the poor design. The A1 saw them treated to an ergonomically designed seat, complete with lumbar support.

An interesting innovation was the installation of equipment that would service the Central Tyre Inflation System (CTIS). The CTIS would allow the front and rear tyres' air pressure to be controlled independently by the driver from the safety and comfort of the cab. Other options included air-conditioning, spare wheel mount as the original didn't carry one as standard, and a driveline protection kit.

No sooner had AM General started work on the A1 than the 1994 Environmental Protection Agency Emissions Update came into force. This essentially killed the stalwart 6.2l diesel engine and so a replacement was sought as a matter of some urgency. Thankfully a replacement was found, the General Engine Products (GEP) 6.5l V8 Optimizer. This new engine produced 160bhp at 3,400rpm and featured a new GM 4L80 automatic gearbox (4F1R). Alongside the new engine larger brakes and half shafts were also fitted along with a strengthened front cross-member. The A2's winches were also upgraded to a Warn Military Pattern 4 winch.

Rear passengers were given new seats and improvements to the suspension system helped smooth the ride. A host of other detailing changes were made including the fitting of CTIS and the tyres were given an updated solid rubber run-flat insert

This M1025 is fitted with CTIS, readily identifiable by the triangular airline protection plate extending from the hub to the rim of the wheel. Easily modelled with a strip of plastic. (A1C Conrad M. Evans)

Amidst the empty 50-cal cases this Dutch-angled shot shows off nicely the gunner's foot plate and the improved seats of this M1100 Armament Carrier. (Chief Mass Communication Specialist Eric A. Clement)

Function check on an M1114 remote-controlled CROWS .50 cal at Salah ad Din Province, Iraq. This M1114 belongs to the 320th Field Artillery Regiment of the 101st Airborne Division (Air Assault). (PH3 (AW) Shawn Hussong, USN)

to replace the previous magnesium alloy type. Arctic heaters can also be fitted for comfort in extreme climates. The M997A2 Ambulance features a patient compartment with white light shut off when the bulkhead or rear doors are opened or when rear steps are deployed.

Delivery started in 1995, which coincided with a more rationalized approached to variant numbering: it was decided to scrap individual numbers for Humvees equipped with winches. Instead of some 17 variants there would now be a mere six:

M1097A2 Troop, Cargo and Shelter Carrier
M1045A2 Up-armoured TOW Carrier
M1025 Armament Carrier Armoured
M1043 Armament Carrier Armoured (USMC)
M997A2 Maxi Ambulance (no winch)
M1035A2 Soft Top Ambulance

The Expanded Capacity Vehicle (ECV)

The next development was the Expanded Capacity Vehicle (ECV), or M1100 series, which had its roots in the experiences of scout elements during the first Gulf War in 1991 as well as peacekeeping duties during 1992 and 1993. The project was once again led by TACOM, who awarded the development contract to vehicle armour specialists O'Gara-Hess & Eisenhardt of Ohio, to produce an 'up-armoured' Humvee. The up-armoured ECV, now referred to as the M1114, would gain over 900kg (2,000lb) in weight as a result of the additional armour, which would include steel-plated doors, steel plating under the cab and several layers of bonded, ballistic-resistant glass for the windows. The extra armour would essentially cocoon the occupants inside the Humvee.

The M1114 could also be refitted with the various upgrades that enhanced underside, side, fuel tank, doors and roof protection. Upgraded gunners' stations, such as the Objective Gunner Protection Kit (OGPK), could also be fitted. Later adaptions included anti-mine and counter-IED devices such as the Self-Protection

Note the mismatched Frag 5 body panels mounted onto this M1114 belonging to the 73rd Cavalry Regiment, photographed at Kir Kush, Diyala Province, Iraq. (SSG Denoris Mickle, USAF)

A USMC M1116 leaves Kandahar Army Air Field (AAF), Kandahar Province, Afghanistan (AFG), to establish Forward Operating Base (FOB) Ripley. (GYSGT Keith A. Milks, USMC)

A wonderful three-quarter shot of a clean M1151; the difference with the initial M1025 is staggering. (Mark Mauno)

Loadmaster Boatswain's Mate 2nd Class Dwayne Todd directs an M1114 with Frag 6 armour, onto a Landing Craft Air Cushion (LCAC) during Exercise Eagle Resolve 2013. Note early wheel rims and D-ring hooks on the corner of the doors to allow easy removal via tow rope. The sand-coloured box at the centre top of the windscreen houses the Blue Force Tracking GPS transmitter. (Mass Communication Specialist 3rd Class Lacordrick Wilson)

Adaptive Roller Kit (SPARK) and the Rhino passive anti-IED device.

A heavier chassis was designed and fitted with improved suspension and an upgraded braking system to cope with the additional weight. Cooling, exhaust and steering systems were improved, which necessitated the extension of the front grille to allow for extra space, giving the series a pronounced snoutish appearance. Also fitted was the same gearbox and 6.5l turbo diesel engine as the A2 versions of the Humvee but these produced 190bhp at 3,400rpm rather than the now-pedestrian 160bhp of the A2.

The M1114 is capable of climbing 40 per cent and traversing a side slope of up to 30 per cent (17 degrees) and can ford hard-bottom water crossings to a depth of up to 0.76m (30in). The M1114 can climb a 460mm (18in) vertical obstacle, and has a 3,090kg (6,820lb) payload.

In late 1995, production of the up-armoured M1114 Armament Carrier began. This platform met the strict requirements for a range of vehicles, including use as an Explosive Ordnance Disposal (EOD) vehicle due to its improved ballistic protection levels, which protect the crew from 7.62mm armour-piercing rounds, 155mm artillery airburst shrapnel and blast from mines containing up to 5.4kg (12lb) of explosive.

In June 1996, the US Army received their first M1114s (390 units) which were used in Bosnia as part of NATO-led Implementation Force (IFOR) and Stabilization Force (SFOR) commitments. By this stage the US Air Force (USAF) saw force protection applications for the M1114, and ordered their own versions, known as the M1116. The M1116 featured an expanded cargo area, armoured housing for the turret gunner, and improved interior air-conditioning. An initial order of 71 units was delivered between February and May 1998; by late 2004 a total of 551 had been delivered to fulfil a variety of roles including Security Police (SP) and Civil Engineer (CE) tasks. Another ECV variant in use with the USAF is the M1145; this offers the same levels of protection as the M1116 for Air Support Operations Squadrons (ASOS) such as Forward Air Control (FAC). A TOW carrier version, the M1121, is also available for use.

The M1151 enhanced armament carrier is an improved version with a heavier chassis and improved General Engine Products (GEP) V8 6.5l turbocharged diesel engine developing 190hp to handle the extra add-on armour. It is built on an Expanded Capacity Vehicle chassis, which allows for more passengers or additional supplies (up to 2,300lb).

The M1152A1 Heavy Cargo/Troop Carrier vehicle replaces previous troop, cargo and shelter carriers in use, including the M1123 and M1097 variants. The M1152A1 is capable of carrying two crew and up to eight passengers in either Armoured Troop Enclosure or Troop Seat configuration.

The M1152A1 can be fitted with the Armor Survivability Kit (ASK) developed by the US Army Research Laboratory (ARL). ASK consists of armoured steel doors with bulletproof glass, protective armoured plating and a ballistic windshield and is available as either a two-door or four-door variant.

A further, heavier, B2 kit is also available, which includes perimeter and overhead armour, and a rear ballistic bulkhead; this kit requires an aluminium roof and rear panel. With the addition of the B2 kit, the M1152A1 provides gapless mine and ballistic protection. These kits are also field installable and removable to provide flexibility. Further upgrades known as Frag 5 or 6 can also be installed. Whilst the details of its material construction remain classified, this spaced armour acts like a spall liner and prevents the vehicle's bodywork acting as a secondary source of fragmentation.

M1165 is a four-person Humvee that can be utilized on a variety of missions, from command and control to armed patrol. It is available with an optional weapons mount and turret and can be readily customized for use by Special Forces.

The M1167 TOW Carrier provides a ring-mounting with a secondary weapons mount for close-range target engagement; the position also gives the gunner a 360° arc of fire. The firing position and gunner is protected by an open-topped ballistic armour turret.

All M1100 series Humvees are considered to have United States Department of the Army (HQDA) Level 1 armour, meaning units are fitted with approved integrated armour with ballistic windows and air-conditioning installed during production/retrofit. It is also considered to provide protection from small arms, mines and IEDs.

Armour Upgrades

At the turn of the twenty-first century the role of US forces engaged in operations in Iraq had changed from conventional warfare to suppressing a growing insurgency. With this new tempo of operations, it became clear that extra armour was urgently required to help deal with the proliferation of IEDs and snap ambushes.

It is universally accepted, no matter the nation, that soldiers have the propensity for adapting to their surroundings. Whilst these adoptions may not always be pretty, they do tend to work. In Iraq Humvees were treated to 'Hillbilly' armour, which consisted of scrap sheet metal supplemented with sandbags with body armour draped on the vehicle sides. The extra protection was negligible, but the weight was not, with suspension and drive train elements failing quickly under the weight. Soon the shortcomings in the Humvee's overall protection were coming under increased criticism from press, troops, families and

US Navy SEALs lay down covering fire from their M1165 as part of an extraction exercise during a capabilities demonstration at Joint Expeditionary Base Little Creek, Va. (Chief Mass Communication Specialist Stan Travioli)

Kin Blue Beach, Japan, 4 September 2014. A Humvee from the 31st Marine Expeditionary Unit (31st MEU) in the US 7th Fleet disembarks a Landing Craft Utility during a scheduled beach raid exercise. (Mass Communication Specialist 1st Class Joshua Hammond)

A shot of USMC Motor Transportation Section, at Camp Fallujah, Al Anbar Province, Iraq. The simple panel armour on the side of the doors and cargo bay is covered with an explosive resistant coating, a sprayed-on Polyurea coating designed to withstand blast pressure. (SGT Chad R. Kiehl, USMC)

An ASK armoured M1114 of the 25th Infantry Division on patrol near Bayji, Iraq. (TSGT Lee Harshman, USAF)

The latest Frag 7 kit is designed to give occupants and gunner superior overhead protection. (Todd Spencer)

Donald Rumsfeld swallowed political pride and reversed an earlier decision to reduce the number of armoured Humvees being produced. Slowly the additional M1100 units and armour kits began appearing in theatre.

In the meantime, the armour kits, including ASK, the ARL-designed stand-off Frag 5 spaced armour fit and the heavy Frag 6 kit, as well as upgrades to the M1151, were filtering through. The ASK was the first to be fitted, in October 2003. This added adding 450kg (1,000lb) to the overall weight of the vehicle. Florida-based armour specialists Armor Holdings soon produced a slightly lighter upgrade kit, that only added an extra 340 kg (750lb).

By the start of 2005 the USMC had got in on the act and had produced the Marine Armor Kit (MAK). Developed by the Marine Corps Systems Command and Marine Corps Logistics Command, MAK offered more protection than the standard M1100 series armour. Unfortunately, it also increased the vehicle weight, so depending on vehicle configuration the extra weight would be between 1,588 and 1,724kg (3,500 and 3,800lb).

In terms of protection the Frag 5 offered increased protection but was inadequate in stopping the effects of EFP attacks. The Frag 6 kit was designed to meet that threat; however, due to its increased bulk it added over 450kg (1,000lb) with an increase in width of 300mm (12in) either side of the vehicle. This extra weight on the doors also presented another problem: the doors jammed shut after being involved in a blast. Again, military ingenuity stepped in and the US Army Aviation and Missile Research, Development, and Engineering Center (AMRDEC) developed the Humvee crew extraction D-ring in 2006. Depending on version, the D-ring is located either

politicians. While some advanced armour protection kits were available, they varied in weight from 680 to 1,000kg (1,500 to 2,200lb) and as a result they had similar drawbacks to the 'Hillbilly' armour.

An upwards blast from a buried IED, or mine, not only defeats conventional/improvised armour but will also destabilize the vehicle, causing further damage and casualties. Another more deadly threat faced by Humvee crews was the increasing use of Explosively Formed Penetrators (EFP) by insurgents. An EFP is a shaped charge that self-forms a warhead post-detonation and is capable of defeating the heaviest of armour.

Most armoured Humvees, the M1100 series in particular, were able to withstand such attacks but their numbers were nowhere near enough to provide the levels of protection needed. Then Defense Secretary

on the lower opening corner of the door, or where the handle would be situated. To open a jammed door one end of a tow strap, chain or cable is simply attached to the D-ring, whilst the other is attached to another vehicle or winch which then pulls the door off.

Another escape device is the Vehicle Emergency Escape (VEE) windows, developed by BAE Systems. The kit does not alter the level of ballistic protection afforded but merely adds a latch feature which allows rapid egress in an emergency. A special rotary latch mechanism with safety interlocks is fitted to the window frame, so that in the event of a vehicle emergency, the two latches are turned and the window is simply pushed out.

The final point of consideration for armour protection was the vulnerable top-cover gunner manning the roof-mounted weapon. To provide protection a basic gun shield or turret was initially fitted. As experience was gained the position developed a high-sided turret complete with bulletproof glass observation panels and on occasion a roof. The very latest Frag 7 kit by Industrial Base Operations- Rock Island Arsenal (IBO-RIA) and AM General Corporation is designed to give enhanced overhead cover (OHC) for gunner and crew.

Aside from the armour upgrades there were necessary changes to cope with the extra weight. These included the introduction of three-piece chassis rails and cross-members, improved engine and power train cooling, handling suspension; braking upgrades as well as redesigned steering.

In 2005 an interesting development to the Humvee was taking place: the composite HMMWV. This was an exercise in weight saving undertaken and developed by US Army Tank Automotive Research, Development and Engineering Center (US TARDEC), TPI Composites, Armor Holdings Inc and AM General. The purpose of the project was to produce a reduced-weight vehicle to enable the carriage of a heavier up-armour kit. When the project was unveiled 18 months later the teams had managed to save approximately 410kg (900lb) compared to the traditional Humvee. Whilst the project didn't lead to any orders, it showed not only what was possible, but opened the door to future collaborative working between TPI Composites and Armor Holdings Inc (later to be bought by BAE Systems).

Recap: The HMMWV Recapitalization Program

At the beginning of the twenty-first century the Humvee had been in service for 15 years. With some 120,000 in service with the US Army and 20,000 in service with the USMC, most had been built during the first six years of production. Initially the standalone Humvee was not expected to serve more than 15 years, or 45,000 miles, a figure calculated by estimating the expected peacetime mileage which would normally be around 3,000 miles per annum. This annual mileage figure was regularly exceeded in a month and, added to this, the M1114 and M1151 variants were experiencing significant increases in operational use as a result of the Global War on Terrorism (GWOT). The M1114 and M1151 variants had also been configured with retrofit capabilities. This meant that converted vehicles were operating beyond their weight limit specifications with the result of increased structural damage. It was also clear that the Humvee would be in service for some years to come.

At the time government funding rules stipulated that any money available was for the purchase of new vehicles only, which could take up to a decade to prove ready for service. In the 1990s the US Army's Product Director Light Tactical Vehicles (PdD LTV) recognized the need to address the rapidly rising Operation and Support (O&S) costs, especially those associated with older vehicles. To that end PbD LTV began to develop an Other Procurement, Army (OPA)-funded programme that would endeavour to upgrade over 100,000 vehicles. The scope of the programme was as breathtaking as it was ambitious; the plan was to return Humvees to almost brand-new condition, which would extend their life and enhance performance for a further 21 years. At the same time O&S costs would also be minimized. The programme would include a host of updated parts as well as a new engine and drive train, with an estimated cost of $40,000 per vehicle.

The extent of the programme expanded in 2000 with the advent of the Army Recapitalization Policy. This initiative aimed to enhance readiness whilst reducing O&S costs by maintaining the average fleet age at or below half the system's expected service life of 15 years. PbD LTV developed a model to predict the average fleet age and numbers of vehicles within service life or over age. This was based on anticipated annual new unit production and unit recapitalization quantities.

As a result, it was determined that some 8,000 vehicles could be recapitalized on an initial annual basis in order meet the desired half-life standard by 2010. The costs were expected to be high and the programme coincided with other recapitalization programmes, which led to further refinements. By late 2001 the proposed programme was deemed not to be cost effective, and as such it was redirected towards an Operations and Maintenance, Army (OMA)-funded project. This would see the original full force project refocus on the recapitalization of older vehicles in III Corps. The engines and drive trains would no longer be replaced, merely rebuilt, whilst each vehicle would be inspected for repairs and component replacement. The Recap Program would

The troop-carrying ETK-T is designed to be driven into a waiting CH-47 as demonstrated here. (AM General)

Behind the automotive glamour is the heart of a proven winner: the NXT 360 is the next step in the Humvee's development. (AM General)

conversions designed to increase mobility, lethality, safety and power. There are eight variants available: the ETK-9 is a nine-personnel transporter type, the ETK-FS fire support platform provides covered seating for eight occupants. The ETK-T, which utilizes the M1097 and M1152, is a special narrow body kit version, tapering upwards so it can be carried by CH-47 Chinook.

The ETK-30 30mm Weapon System uses the M1151 and features an Integrated Gunner Protection Kit (GPK) providing an open turret carrying the LW 30mm M230LF (link-fed) chain gun. The ETK-I roof-mounted TOW missile Humvee platform is based on the M1167 and is fitted with a twin TOW missile launcher. ETK-A is an autonomous Humvee platform which provides the remote user with vital visual information. The ETK-A also carries a tethered UAS, stored on the rear cargo deck, for aerial reconnaissance. The ETK-MC mission command and control M1152-based shelter carrier can accommodate four command and control specialists in a climate-controlled environment.

The final vehicle of the ETK range is the ETK-P power platform which is designed to provide up to 30kW of electrical power via generators mounted behind the crew cab body on the cargo bed. All are based on the M1097 and M1152 and feature crush protection and integrated passenger restraints.

Another development is the NXT 360, an off-the-shelf purchase or upgrade option for armament carrier M1100 Humvees, which provides enhanced protection against the kinetic energy generated by blast through blast mats fitted underneath the crew area, protected seating and exterior armour plating.

With the additional weight the NXT 360's suspension has improved, and increased tyre size helps traction and decrease ground pressure. There is greater ground clearance, improved ride and an increase in the approach and departure angles. Anti-lock Brake System (ABS) and Electronic Stability Control (ESC) traction control is also fitted. Power comes from a P400 electronically controlled 6.5l 250hp multi-fuel (Avtur, petrol or diesel) V8 turbocharged engine linked to a 6L85e six-speed automatic transmission unit.

These developments show that, like the British Land Rover, the Humvee may not be the ideal platform for asymmetrical warfare but it is a formidable vehicle. Despite its gradual frontline replacement by the Oshkosh series of Joint Light Tactical Vehicles (JLTVs) the Humvee remains in service around the world. However, the Humvee story is far from over, with the vehicle expected to remain in service with the US military until 2050. Added to this there is its global use and numerous upgrade options from a host of manufacturers, proving there is plenty of life left in the iconic Humvee.

deliver a vehicle with a ten-year extended service life. This rewritten programme was approved by the Vice Chief of Staff of the Army (VCSA) on 19 October 2001 with initial funding for the recapitalization of 4,372 total vehicles starting in 2004.

The Recap Program was a watershed moment for the Humvee; it saw older M998s and M1037s rebuilt into sturdier M1097R1 heavy shelter carriers that could also carry additional armour. It was also an opportunity to embed new technology into the Humvee fleet, the main piece being a new power train which would deliver improved reliability and range. The results were impressive and soon M1038s and older M1097s were recapped to M1097R1 standard. Another version was the M1025R1 Armament Carrier which was created from M1025 and M1026, both original and A1 versions.

By 2011 five contractors, including AM General, had successfully worked on the Recap Program delivering over 46,000 vehicles. At this time the pilot of the M1151A1 Recapitalization Pilot Program had completed 340 vehicles and became known as the Modernized Expanded Capacity Vehicle (MECV) program. In 2012, as a result of budget cuts and a shift in focusing on developing the Joint Light Tactical Vehicle (JLTV), the MECV program's Recap funding was cancelled.

A further development by AM General are the Enhanced Tactical Kit (ETK)

Humvee in Detail

Aside from the expected technological and mechanical improvements, the basic Humvee has changed little. This makes the Humvee a wonderful vehicle to model, with the design broken down into three basic types: the two-crew pickup, the crew-cab pickup and the hard-bodied weapon carrier. Externally very little has changed aside from the up-armoured M1100 expanded capacity vehicle series.

Starting from the front of the Humvee the most notable aspect is the front grille with vertical bars. On early production A1 and A2 models the grille sits, along with the headlights, flush to the front edge of the bonnet. The M1100 series sees the grille and headlights protrude forwards, which makes this a great recognition feature. Where fitted the Warn winch cable is attached to the front cross-member and sits within a steel housing, fed through a forward-facing aperture. The housing sits forward of the grille on all models aside from the M1100 series, where it is flush with the grille. On earlier versions the Warn winch was electrically powered, but this was changed to be hydraulically driven, drawing power from the power-steering pump.

A brush guard is a frequent addition to the Humvee; this folds forward to enable the bonnet to be opened. When closed the bonnet is held in place by two sturdy rubber straps located behind the wheel arches. The engine bay is a cramped affair, and a plumber's nightmare, the V8 engine mounted behind the front axle partially disappearing beneath the front window. The large radiator sits ahead of the engine and is set at an angle to allow a low bonnet profile. Either side of the radiator sits the chassis-mounted helicopter sling attachment points for airmobile operations, which in turn protrude through the bonnet. The rear sling points are positioned on the rear bumper or for USMC Humvees, which eschew a rear bumper, on the ends of the longitudinal chassis beams. All chassis, suspension and drive train elements are painted matt black during manufacture. Underneath the rear cross-member, attached to a flip-down rack, are the pioneer tools which include a spade, axe, mattock head and handle. The rack is hinged and held in place with a couple of latches, which, when released, swing down to enable access.

To the left of the engine sits a large cylindrical air filter to which a snorkel can be attached for deep-water use. It's common to see the snorkel, with the side-mounted raised exhaust, retained in place on USMC

A wonderful view of the chassis looking from the bumper; of note is the rear winch and slightly skewed engine fitting.

Brush guard in lowered position with the bonnet raised. (Dieter Krause)

Here the anti-debris baffle is visible along with the sling points either side of the radiator. Note the rubber stops to prevent damage to the bonnet should it accidently drop. (Dieter Krause)

vehicles. On the opposite side of the engine sits the large alternator, surrounded by various fluid reservoirs, which can be a 60, 100 or 200Ah 24V unit depending on type of Humvee.

The interior is an austere affair painted in either NATO Green or Sand throughout with seating covers in a range of colours from olive green to khaki, dependent on age and manufacturer. The split front windscreen, which can be fitted with either polycarbonate or reinforced glass units, can be lowered forward over the bonnet and is held in place with a split pin. On the extreme left of the dashboard sits the M-series light switch, a common feature on US military vehicles from the 1950s until its replacement from 2002 with a push-button LED-illuminated control panel. The Humvee features all the usual military lights including blackout, as well as side reflectors and side-clearance lights.

Above the light switch is the keyless three-position starting lever. To operate the driver turns the starting lever from STOP to RUN, waits for the coil warmup light situated above the switch to extinguish before rotating the lever to START. Immediately to the right of this sits the air filter flow gauge. The steering wheel is not as big as expected for a vehicle of this size, a mere 355mm in diameter, with the horn pad mounted in its centre. A single indicator and hazard switch lever are attached to the steering column. Underneath the dashboard is a thick self-retracting cable and lock which threads through the steering wheel to prevent unauthorized use. A small fire extinguisher is placed in the recess between the driver's seat and the side panel.

The main instrument panel includes speedo, fuel levels and engine temperature gauges; to the right sit rudimentary environment controls for hot and cold air. The windscreen wipers are controlled via a simple twist switch mounted on the windscreen frame, which allows the driver or passenger to control the wipers. The handbrake and transmission controls sit on the left side of the transmission tunnel, above which, when fitted, sits the radio tray for the SINCGARS radio set and ancillaries. Later models are fitted with the Force XXI Battle Command Brigade and Below communication platform, Blue Force Tracking GPS and a Digital Command and Control System LCD screen. These are attached to the SINCGARS' right-hand side with the screen on a swing mount. Vehicle batteries are found underneath the passenger seat and are accessed by removing the seat pad.

In the armament carrier versions, the gunner accesses weapons via a single-piece hinged roof hatch. On early carriers the weapons mounts were turned by the gunner's weight. As the armour increased and turrets got heavier, e.g. M1114, a hand crank was introduced. On ECV Humvees the weight is such that the turret is turned by an electric motor. Initially the gunner stood on a scissor-sprung platform fitted to the transmission cover that could be raised or lowered as required. By the first decade of the new century a sling seat, which hangs from the turret ring, was introduced to replace adapted webbing yolks and straps. Where fitted the rear seats can fold down to increase stowage space.

The Humvee's driver position is spartan to say the least. Note the rifle barrel clip by the door, and the anti-theft security cable lashed around the steering wheel. (Dieter Krause)

The driver's seat and extinguisher; note the 180° swing on the driver's door hinge and transmission tunnel soundproofing. (Dieter Krause)

Storekeeper 2nd Class Eddie Burgos and Intelligence Specialist 2nd Class Mike Tomazin enjoy a refresh with the Humvee, an excellent shot showing the frugal dashboard and SINCGARS radio mount. (Photographer's Mate Airman Brian Goodwin)

Humvee in Detail 21

A turret sling fitted to a USAF M1151 at Joint Base Balad, Iraq, 2009. Note the back padding and electronic turret power control box attached to the turret ring. (Dainomite)

SGT Shann Snyder hangs in his seatbelt while SGT Glen Naylor works himself free during training in the Humvee Egress Assistance Trainer at Fort Harrison, Montana. This shot shows the unique shape of the turret opening and the hatch stays. (US Army)

View from above showing the Objective Gunner Protection Kit (O-GPK) turret. Note the folded sunshade and barbed wire bale on the trunk. (Todd Huffman)

A well-worn gunner's platform; the colour would be best replicated by a bronze/brown mix. (Dieter Krause)

A great shot of an early M1097 on manoeuvres with full SINCGARS rig; even better for the modeller is the plastic-covered door showing the zipped-down window held in place by the simple expedient of tucking it behind the forming frame. (Dieter Krause)

An interior shot of the rear cargo area of an early M1025 showing the opening latch, by the black handle, for swinging the truck door backward to allow access to stores, a great asset for the TOW carrier. (Ciacho)

M1025 cargo bay showing the various strapping which ensure stores are secured. Clockwise from left wheel arch: jerrycan stowage next to which is ammo box stowage, padded M2 stowage and tripod stowage closest to the bay edge. Note the NATO Brown overspray on bay floor. (Dieter Krause)

Looking down towards the cockpit of this M998 in troop carrier setup is a revelation. Note the folded rear seats with seat pads stowed on top, the rear door blanking plates and the interesting arrangement of radio equipment next to the driver. The side seats echo the simple design ethos that AM General adopted for the Humvee from the start. (Don Busack)

On the early Humvees, doors were simple metal frames covered with plastic-coated nylon, complete with zip-down windows that kept the dirt out. The armament carriers and ambulances were fitted with Kevlar-reinforced doors, easily identifiable by the cross moulded into the door's surface to provide rigidity. As the development of the Humvee continued, later versions with appliqué armour started to appear.

The sloped rear of the armament carrier is a door capable of opening from either the top or the bottom. The ability to open from the top is useful for the TOW carrier as it gives the gunner access to replacement rounds without recourse to exit the vehicle. When opening from the bottom the tailgate can also be lowered as per the basic version. The tailgate can be utilized to carry rolled camouflaged netting, or extra fuel and water via Gypsy Racks. A body-mounted swing spare tyre mount can also be fitted.

Camouflage is applied both on the assembly, in the field and, in the case of theatre-mounted armour kits, at place of manufacture. This can often lead to vehicles displaying panels of different colours, as well as some interesting wear patterns. For those vehicles based in arctic regions camouflage is simply diluted white emulsion applied over the vehicle with a paintbrush. The normal camouflage is three-tone NATO for temperate areas, and either sand or tan for desert environments. A great way to age the Humvee is to count the outer ring of nuts on the wheels, which changed with model development: the fewer there are the older the vehicle.

Key Modelling Essentials

The Humvee is straightforward in terms of appearance, very little having changed over the years. These pointers will guide you towards making your authentic build, be it patrolling the deserts of South West Asia or the Arctic wastes of NATO's northern flank:

- Early production Humvees have the manufacturer's name embossed into the rear tailgate.
- The chassis and power train are painted black on the AM General production line; any other colour is a change after the vehicle has been taken on at unit level.
- The engine is mounted slightly off-centre, so when placing the block in the chassis, it should reflect this.
- The clamshell trunk can be opened from either the rear or the front, and when parked the bonnet is often raised to prevent sunlight glancing off the windscreen and giving away the vehicle's position.
- Humvees used on winter exercises are often brush-painted with a rough and heavy whitewash stripe finish.
- SFOR/IFOR markings came in a range of sizes and finishes and was applied

Humvee in Detail

The rear antenna mount is fully flexible as shown on this M1097. (Dieter Krause)

Pioneer tools in travelling position on this early M998. (Don Busack)

with simple off-the-shelf spray cans which often resulted in overspray, especially on the soft-door versions.
- Combat Identification Panels (CIPs) hung either on the doors or the side rear panels and over the front grille when in use.
- In-theatre vehicles often carried rolls of barbed wire on the bonnet, or the rear truck cover of the armament versions. Occasionally a camouflage net or light tent would be attached to the tailgate.
- There are two differing bonnet grilles, the earlier type featuring fewer bars compared to those on the bonnets of the later M1100 series.
- Up-armoured vehicles, especially in the desert theatres, often have mismatched panels as a result of additional armour installation or panel replacement due to damage in theatre.
- USMC Humvees often retain their snorkels and high-mounted exhaust pipes, regardless of location; remember to remove rear bumpers too.

Specifications

Whilst there are a host of HMMWV Humvee variants, I have chosen to share the specifications of the M998/M1038 platforms.

M998/M1038 HMMWV Specifications

Production period: 1984–present.
Body/chassis: Welded box-section steel ladder chassis with riveted and bonded aluminium, with GRP panelled body over aluminium frame.
Engine: General Motors Detroit Diesel Allison (DDA) liquid-cooled V8.
Cubic capacity: 6,227cc (6,555cc in vehicles produced from 1994).
Horsepower: 6,227cc: 150bhp at 3,600rpm / 6,555cc: 160bhp at 4,000rpm / 6,555cc turbo-diesel: 190bhp at 3,400rpm.
Transmission: General Motors GM3L80 3-Speed Turbo-Hydramatic: 3F1Rx2 auto (1984–94) & GM4L80E 4 Speed Turbo-Hydramatic: 4F1Rx2 auto (1995 onwards) driving portal gear hubs for all four wheels.
Steering and suspension: Power-assisted Saginaw 708 variable ratio (13/16:1) steering unit. Independent 4x4, double A-arms on coil springs with hydraulic double acting shock absorbers.
Brakes: Inboard hydraulic front and rear discs with hydraulic boost, with rear disc mechanical parking brake.
Electrical systems: 2–12V standard, 24V for radio-equipped versions.
Dimensions:
Track: 72in (1.83m)
Wheelbase: 130in (3.3m)
Total length: 184in (4.67m)/ 186in (4.72m)
Overall width: 86in (2.19m)
Height: 72in (1.37m) to top of windscreen
Dry weight: 5,200lb (2,360kg)/5,327lb (2,418kg)
Ground clearance: 16in (0.41m)

Plywood strengthening board in place; note the Velcro strapping for keeping the tilt in place over the ceiling frame and the windscreen wiper control knob top-centre of the windscreen. (Dieter Krause)

24 HUMVEE

USMC return from a patrol through the Bel Air area of Port-au-Prince, Haiti, as part of Operation Secure Tomorrow 2004. Note lack of rear bumper. (LCPL Kevin Mccall, USMC)

No 53 Marine LCPL Daniel Quiroz guarding United Nations trucks, loaded at Biadoa Air Field for feeding centres in Somalia, 1993. This is a great view of an early Humvee; note side mirrors and lights especially. (PH1 R. J. Oriez)

An interesting shot of a rare occurrence: the rear cab cover in place. A vast amount of detail here to soak up and enjoy. (Dieter Krause)

A great shot of the raised bonnet showing that even the professionals leave marks when finishing their camouflage. (Dieter Krause)

In Service & In Action

Left: A USMC M1097 negotiating a water obstacle in Khowst Province, Afghanistan. Note the abundance of stores required to ensure mission effectiveness. (CPL James L. Yarboro, USMC)

Below: Operation Uphold Democracy. Soldiers warn occupants of a targeted building, using a psychological operations speaker, to evacuate. These speakers were used to wear down Noriega using the music of Rick Astley in 1989. (SPC Jean-Marc Schaible)

The Humvee is the third generation of US military light utility trucks to see active service since World War II. The platform was a welcome return to the go-anywhere-do-anything ethos of its predecessor, the Jeep, and the Humvee soon became the GI's new best friend. Since its introduction, the Humvee has taken on its everyman role with enviable ease. This ease has been battle-proven time and again, from the jungles of Central America to the deserts of South West Asia. The Humvee's first major operational deployment and public outing was in Operation Just Cause, Panama, 1989. This was also the first major outing of the sleeker US military and a test of the lighter mechanized infantry concept that the Humvee was envisaged to be part of.

In the early hours of 20 December 1989, 26,000 troops left their line of departure with the aim of apprehending the dictator General Manuel Noriega and installing democratically elected Guillermo Endara as president. Used as a softer force-projection asset, the Humvee could transport troops, who were stationed at Southern Command training facilities, quickly into urban environments where tracked vehicles would be deemed unsuitable to use.

From 21 December Southern Commands Psyops Humvees were placed around the Vatican Embassy where Noriega had sought refuge where they played music through vehicle-mounted speakers 24 hours a day. The tunes came from requests made by troops and included 'Welcome to the Jungle' by Guns 'n' Roses and 'Never gonna give you up' by Rick Astley. By way of a change on Christmas Day festive music was played, with rock music returning on 26 December. On 3 January Noriega surrendered.

While the operation had been a success for the Humvee, comments were made by the 6th Infantry Regiment regarding the lack of personnel protection offered by the

A soldier reverses a M998 Communications vehicle at the new location of the 2nd Armored Cavalry Regiment during Operation Desert Storm. (SPC Faas)

A mass of detail here as personnel prepare to move out during Operation Desert Storm. (SPC Elliott)

UNPROFOR M1025s belonging to the 1st Armored Division wait at Outpost U-51B in the hills of northern Macedonia. (SSG John E. Lasky)

vehicle. Several ides were mooted, including sandbags, but the key area requiring protection was the roof gunner. Like the M113 ACAV 25 years before, the Humvee's gunner needed protection, so a similar design was made to protect the gunner from incoming fire.

In 1990 the Humvee made its first appearance in the motor pool of a foreign power at a victory parade held by the Union for the Total Independence of Angola (UNITA) forces as a 106mm portee. As the US was not directly involved in Angola's long civil war, it's highly likely the Humvees on parade were part of a covert CIA support package. While seemingly innocuous, it showed there was an appetite for the Humvee from overseas buyers.

On 2 August 1990, Iraqi forces invaded the Kingdom of Kuwait, and by the time of Operation Desert Storm, 16 January 1991, the Humvee was supporting the advancing formations. On the night of 23/24 February the ground offensive started and the Humvee set off with the armour. The advancing Humvees, squat, powerful and overloaded with huge amounts of personal kit, reflected the troops' aggressive nature and desire for a fight against the Iraqis.

Within 100 hours the war was over, with the Humvee passing its main test – prolonged exposure to heavy loads, heat, abrasive sand and plenty of cross-country action. As a result of its use in the field many of the coalition partners, including Kuwait, were keenly eying up the Humvee as a replacement for their own light truck fleets.

By the end of 1991 the Cold War was literally history, and the desire to field more Motorized Divisions waned with the threat once posed by the likes of the Soviet 254th Motor Rifle Division and the East German 1st Motorized Rifle Division. The New World Order that Bush had promoted in his post-Operation Desert Storm speech saw the US military step up their humanitarian interventions. The first big test came in 1992 when the UN operation in Somalia (UNOSOM) came under increasing attack from local clans whilst delivering humanitarian aid.

In December 1992, President Bush allocated to the UN 25,000 troops to help secure lines of communication under the banner Operation Restore Hope and by March 1993 Somalia had stabilized enough for the UN to take over the task. Whilst the overall mission was successful, the fragility of the Humvee was exposed with several damaged or destroyed by small-arms fire and improvised explosive devices.

Closer to home the UN mission in Haiti (UNMIH) that had been established to restore president-elect Jean-Bertrand Aristide, who'd been overthrown in a coup d'état in 1991, as well as modernize certain aspects of Haitian military. By 1994 it was felt the military authorities were not acting in the best interests of the country; the situation was politically complex and highly volatile. In September a diplomatic mission led by President Jimmy Carter showed a video-feed of the 82nd Airborne Division being loaded onto aircraft to coup leader General Cédras which convinced him to reassess the situation. He readily capitulated. Whilst the majority of the 82nd didn't make landfall, as they were no longer required, the 10th Mountain Division did, who soon started to secure the peace and reorganize vital services.

One key role the Humvee carried out was delivering literature and broadcasting messages via mounted loudspeakers with Joint Psychological Operations Task Force (JPOTF). Not only did this provide the local population with consistent information, it also provided effective information to friendly forces, acting as a useful eyes and ears on the ground.

On the other side of the Atlantic diplomacy had failed in the former Yugoslavia, with the Slovenes and Croats leaving the federation in 1991. The situation in Bosnia was more complex and an unofficial referendum was held by the Serb minority in new Republic of Bosnia-Herzegovina. As a result of the referendum the ethnic Serbs declared a new state, *Republika Srpska*, allied to Yugoslavia main, and separate from Bosnia. This new proto-state effectively drove a wedge through the geographic centre of Bosnia–Herzegovina, aggravating ethnic Croats and Bosnians.

The UN soon became involved operating as UN Protection Force (UNPROFOR) which was accused of doing very little outside of aid delivery, most notably the lack of intervention in the Srebrenica massacre. Humvees soon began to make appearances in the white UN peacekeeping livery around key points and settlements. However, peacekeepers on the ground often found their hands tied, or worse still, targets of deliberate attack by ethnic Serbs.

By 1995 the situation was out of control, and in August the US sent former diplomat Richard Holbrooke as special envoy to negotiate a new peace deal, which culminated in the Dayton Agreement. Signed on 14 December, the multifaceted agreement saw NATO take over security of Bosnia–Herzegovina from the UN and a new Implementation Force (IFOR) commenced a year-long mandate to bring about stabilization. The first task was to separate opposing forces, moving heavy weaponry to special locations, and patrol an 870-mile internal border between the Serbs and Bosnians. Whilst completing these tasks vital infrastructure and civil engineering works were also undertaken, including reopening Sarajevo airport.

With 60,000 troops at its disposal, NATO had the military might to make a real difference, and bring normality back to the civilian population. US troops would be working alongside former Cold War adversaries, the Russians, who were back

A member of Task Force Eagle on watch in a Bosnian town. (SSG Louis Briscese, USAF)

An M998 awaits its driver at Tuzla Air Base. (SSG David W. Richards)

on familiar ground. The lessons learned in Panama, Somalia and Haiti showed that a large tracked vehicle was not the best way to reassure third parties that they weren't a conquered nation. The Humvee reassured a damaged and scared population, but it still had the mass to portray itself as an iron fist in a velvet glove to those who wished their neighbours harm. The Humvee was also the tool of choice for transportation in the region, given the poor state of many of the roads. Tracked vehicles were more of a hazard in damaging roads and being unable to

Polish troops from the Civil Military Cooperation Group at Camp Echo providing security on the Hwaeer road, Iraq. (USAF)

traverse some of the narrower rural tracks. Humvees became a regular sight, travelling throughout the US sector in the north of the country, with special secure boxes carried in the rear of the vehicles to hold confiscated weapons. Overall, these boxes did their job well, often carrying explosive devices that were over 40 years old, though occasionally there was the odd, non-lethal, mishap.

Humvees had the IFOR and later Stabilization Force (SFOR December 1996– December 1998) markings sprayed on their sides in white. For the modeller there was no standardization, and signage reflects local conditions, sometimes neat and tidy, others looking like they had been applied with a roller. The most common type of Humvee used was the M1025 Armaments Carrier version often mounting an M60. A roll of barbed wire, for use in impromptu roadblocks, was also carried on the rear trunk, and Combat Identification Panels (CIPs) were also mounted, on occasion two square reflective panels, ¾ yellow/¼ red, were placed on the lower part of the trunk. In June 1999 the Humvee was on the move again to support the UN and NATO mandates in the now autonomous region of Kosovo – again fulfilling the same role it was doing in Bosnia.

In 1996 the newly introduced M1113 Expanded Capacity Vehicle (ECV) family of Humvees began supporting NATO mandates as well as US interests overseas. The M1114 saw service with SFOR and KFOR (Kosovo Force) whilst the air-conditioned USAF up-armoured M1116 Armament Carrier found itself working the large US air bases in Saudi Arabia and Kuwait.

Its big test was to come with the dawn of the new millennium and the events of 9 September 2001. Like its British counterpart, the Land Rover, most Humvees were soft skinned, designed for a war that would, in the main, be fought far away from where it was being used. It would be its almost unparalleled off-road ability that would thrust it into a frontline that was as unpredictable as it was dangerous.

By the time of the Iraqi invasion nearly 10,000 Humvees were in theatre providing support for Operation Iraqi Freedom (OIF) and Operation Enduring Freedom (OEF). The US, and others, had hoped to use the Humvee in the same sort of role as it had been used during Balkans operations, where losses would be the exception not the norm. Used as the more acceptable face of internal security, able to traverse poor roads and narrow streets, the very aspects that made the Humvee ideal were its downfall. Sadly, nearly all were the standard M998/M1025 soft-skinned types and due to the nature of an increasingly asymmetric conflict, were exposed to IEDs that could flip a 60-ton tank. Combined with regular ambushes, the standard Humvees stood little chance.

The use of locally produced 'Hillbilly' armour became widespread: from extra sandbags, metal sheeting and flak jackets draped over doors, it tried to alleviate damage and loss of life. These local and frequently heavy solutions often caused damage to drive trains and suspension. By 2004 add-on armour packages were being produced by Army Research Lab, who produced the Armor Survivability Kit (ASK). Armor Holdings Inc and the US Marine Corps also produced armour packages. The USMC kit, the Marine Armour Kit (MAK), added up to 1,545kg to the overall weight of the M1043; already fitted with supplemental armour, it became commonplace. On top of these changes there was a need for air-conditioning and some 6,000 Red Dot air-conditioning units were ordered to keep troops cool in their newly armoured cocoons.

However, casualties continued increasing. Mounting public and political concerns in the US as to whether or not the Humvee was suitable led to the development of an appropriate replacement, the Joint Light Tactical Vehicle (JLTV). In the interim more suitable vehicles such as the Cougar Mine Resistant Ambush Protected (MRAP) were purchased, with the Humvee slowly returning to support roles.

Commandant of the Marine Corps General James T. Conway looks over the Humvee capsule with Marine Corps Warfighting Lab personnel at Quantico; this was soon overshadowed by the arrival of the Cougar and similar MRAPs. (DoD)

Humvee Variants

Like many wheeled tactical vehicles, it's true to say that a huge range of variants has grown around the Humvee Family of Vehicles (FOV), from classified SIGINT (signals intelligence) radio communications vehicles to specialist air defence vehicles. Add to this list impromptu field modifications and the scope for the modeller is unparalleled. The following isn't an exhaustive list, but provides details of versions likely to be of interest to the modeller.

Shop Equipment, Contact Maintenance (SECM)
The SECM is a light engineering support vehicle which carries a mobile workshop capable of fulfilling minor mechanical engineer and repair work.

An Iraqi Army SECM Humvee in Baghdad, Iraq. This was procured by the Iraqi Ministry of Defence through the foreign military sales programme. (CAPT David F. Roy)

The AN/TSC-93A/B and 156 Tactical SHF Satellite Terminal (TSST)
The AN/TSC-156 Phoenix Tactical SHF Satellite Terminal (TSST) is a sizeable piece of communications equipment that requires two Humvee shelter carriers for transportation and use. When in use the dish is mounted atop one of the Humvees, though due to its size, when not in use, the dish is transported on a sizeable trailer behind the mounting unit.

A Tactical Satellite Communication System (AN-TSC 93B), mounted on a High Mobility Multipurpose Wheeled Vehicle (HMMWV), operated and maintained by the New York-based Marine Reserve, 6th Communications Battalion, in support of Baltic Challenge '97. (LCPL E. J. Young)

AN/MLQ-40(V) Prophet Electronic Attack (EA) and Electronic Support (ES) Architecture
Prophet is a tactical signals intelligence (SIGINT) and electronic warfare (EW) suite capable of detecting and locating enemy communications from a range of sources. Mounted on a crew cab Humvee, the system can also locate unattended ground sensors.

Ground Sensor Surveillance Vehicle (GSSV) M1165
Mounted on the M1165 crew cab variant, the GSSV is a classified intelligence-gathering platform used by the US Navy's Space and Naval Warfare Systems Command. It is the Sensor Mobile Monitoring System (SMMS) subsystem of the USMC's Tactical Remote Sensor System (TRSS).

US Navy OS2 Roland Reed in a GSSV is assigned to the Mobile Inshore Undersea Warfare Unit 105, tracks surface contacts, to provide seaward surveillance and security to friendly forces. (JO2 Brian Brannon, USN)

M707 Striker aka M707 Knight HMMWV
The M707 Striker Humvees were typically assigned to a Combat Observation Lasing Team (COLT) for fire support command and control as well as night observation by utilizing a modified armaments carrier cupola fitted with a Ground Vehicular Laser Locator Designator (G/VLLD).

M998 Avenger
Armed with eight FIM-92 Stinger missiles and a .50-cal machine gun, the M998 Avenger Air Defence System (ADS) variant is a bit of an oddity in the Humvee FOV as it is not strictly classed as a Humvee, regardless of the fact that the system is mounted on one. Avenger is designed to provide ground-based, short-range mobile air-defence solutions against a range of airborne targets including low-flying aircraft and is used solely by the US Military. Avenger is available in three configurations: the Basic, Slew-to-Cue, and the Up-Gun. The basic configuration consists of a

gyro-stabilized air defence turret carrying two launcher pods, each capable of rapidly firing up to four fire-and-forget infrared/ultraviolet guided missiles. The Avenger can also be linked to the Forward Area Air Defence Command, Control, Communications and Intelligence (FAAD C3I) system. This allows the passage of mission-vital information to be sent to the system gunner. The Slew-to-Cue (STC) subsystem allows selection of an FAAD C3I target from a display on a targeting console. Once the target has been selected, the turret will automatically slew to the target.

Corporal Theodore Clay, USMC, 1st Stinger Battery, Okinawa, Japan, performs routine maintenance on an Avenger weapons system, before taking it into the field at Shoalwater Bay training area, Queensland, Australia, during Exercise Crocodile. (LCPL Ryan T. Ledoux)

Humvee-mounted Active Denial System (ADS)
The Active Denial System is a non-lethal directed-energy crowd-control device developed by the US Military and can be mounted on a Humvee. It is nicknamed the 'Heat Ray' on account of its reported effects on the body which leave the targeted individual feeling as though they've been exposed to a source of heat. The ADS system looks like a large radar dish atop a shelter when deployed, with the operator sitting in a specially designed control room behind the cab where they can activate the system against a target identified via a TV screen. Although deployed to Afghanistan, the system was not used.

Active Denial System, a non-lethal weapon mounted on the Humvee for crowd control.

The Ground Mobility Vehicle (GMV)
The Ground Mobility Vehicle (GMV) is a US Special Operations Command (USSOCOM) variant based on the M1025 or M1113 chassis. A further version, based on the M1165 chassis, can be fitted with additional armour to create an up-armoured GMV which can include an optional ballistic shield around the gunner's turret. The GMV has a range of 275 miles (443km) and a maximum speed of 70mph (110kph) and features an exposed cargo bay to enable easy storage of mission-relevant stores and personal equipment. Capable of carrying ten troops, the GMV can operate away from main bases for up to ten days.

Several variants are currently in use: the GMV-S (Army Special Forces), the GMV-R (75th Ranger Regiment), GMV-N (Navy SEALs), GMV-T/GMV-SD/GMV-ST (Air Force Special Operations Command (AFSOC) variants), and the GMV-M (United States Marine Forces Special Operations Command MARSOC variant). The Danish-operated Humvee-based Jülkat was similar in appearance and role to the GMV.

The Ground Mobility Vehicle (GMV) provides flexibility and can be deployed in a variety of ways including airdrop, air–land and air-insertion. (DoD)

Jülkat, the Danish armoured HMMWV (retrofitted with add-on composite armour kit) in Afghanistan.

The Integrated Meteorological System (IMETS)
The Integrated Meteorological System (IMETS) was developed by Northrop Grumman to act as the meteorological component of the Intelligence and Electronic Warfare (IEW) element of the Army Battle Command System (ABCS). It is a fully mobile, tactical and automated weather data receiving, processing and dissemination system operated by a US Air Force weather team using the Army-furnished and maintained system.

Republic of China IMET on show at Gangshan Air Force Base. (Gen Fumio)

Zeus

The Humvee-mounted Zeus HMMWV Laser Ordnance Neutralization, or ZEUS-HLONS, is a solid-state laser weapon that was initially a cooperative effort between Sparta Inc and Naval Explosive Ordnance Disposal Technology Division (NAVEODTECHDIV) to destroy unexploded ordnance. The main method deployed to neutralize surface landmines and other threats is a 0.5kW commercial solid state laser (SSL); the associated beam control system is mounted on the rear of a Humvee. In 2003 the system was deployed to Afghanistan where it neutralized 211 items of recovered and discovered Russian ordnance of varying types. Fifty-one items were destroyed in a single 100-minute period, setting a new record for this type of ordnance disposal.

Zeus using its solid state laser to dispatch an identified target in Afghanistan, Note the shattered Soviet-era material and safe route markers either side of the cleared track. (US Army Space and Missile Defense Command)

Surface Launched Advanced Medium-Range Air-to-Air Missile (SLAMRAAM)

The M1152-mounted SLAMRAAM system is intended to operate side by side with Avenger units and not act as a direct replacement, carrying four AIM-120 Advanced Medium-Range Air-to-Air Missiles (AMRAAM) launched from a rear ramp. It provides protection at both short and medium ranges from air asset attack with missiles receiving their guidance information from externally located radar.

The SLAMRAAM ready to deploy. Note the armoured cab, probably not the most comfortable place to sit when the missiles are launched. (Cindy Farmer)

Humvee VISMOD

There are two main Visual Modification (VISMOD) versions of the Humvee currently in use. The first is a BRDM (Boyevaya Razvedyvatelnaya Dozornaya Mashina) version achieved by a simple sheet metal-covered frame to the front portion of an armament carrier. The second transforms the Humvee into either a T-72 or BTR-90 using a multimedia kit, fake turret and reshaped bodywork hung from a frame. VISMODs are equipped with gas-operated weapon systems that simulate the firing of .50-calibre and 125mm main guns. These guns are also linked to the Multiple Integrated Laser Engagement System (MILES) and are fitted with a smoke generator. VISMODs enable soldiers to practise battlefield tactics without using real AFVs which are expensive to run.

Lieutenant Eziezynski from the 177th Armoured Brigade waits for his moment to strike. (Jeff Mellody/US Army)

Common Remotely Operated Weapon Station (CROWS)

The armament carrier Common Remotely Operated Weapon Station (CROWS) system is controlled by the gunner seated safely in the interior of the vehicle, controlling the weapon via a conventional joystick. The mount, which can accept a range of weapons including the Mk 19 grenade launcher, has a 360-degree rotation and -20 to +60-degree elevation and is gyrostabilized. The gunner's sight package includes a daylight video and thermal cameras as well as an eye-safe laser rangefinder. To complete the system, CROWS is fitted with a fully integrated fire-control system that provides ballistic correction as necessary.

Boomerang

Boomerang is an anti-sniper acoustic detection system that uses seven microphone sensors, affixed to a roof-mounted pole, which detect and measure muzzle blast and the supersonic shock wave from a travelling round. Each microphone detects the sound at slightly different times, enabling an onboard computer to calculate the direction, height and range of the shooter in less than a second. The system operator receives almost simultaneous visual and auditory information on the point of fire from an internally mounted LED 12-hour clock image display panel and speaker mounted inside the vehicle. The speaker provides audio confirmation of the location of the shooter whilst the computer gives the range, elevation and azimuth.

Overseas Variants

The Humvee has become a military and social icon as well as a commercial success, with over 30 countries welcoming the light utility vehicle into their motor transport pools. Nations such as Oman and Taiwan bought their Humvees via the U.S. Foreign Military Sales programme, whilst some, such as Iraq, have received theirs as gifts. Other countries such as Georgia and Latvia have been able to purchase directly from AM General. Some countries build the marque under licence from AM General. Greek Humvees, for example, are built by Thessaloniki-based Hellenic Vehicle Industry (ELVO), who have produced six versions. These include general-purpose and ambulance versions as well as an armament carrier which can be fitted with a Russian 9M133 Kornet anti-tank guided missile or the Heckler & Koch GMG40 automatic grenade launcher. For the modeller, the only

The Hamer Orev is the Israeli TOW carrier, seen here on manoeuvres with a Merkava fitted with an anti-tank mine roller. (Matanya)

A Greek Army M1114GR vehicle with weapon mount capable of carrying a Russian 9M133 Kornet ATGM firing post. Note the single-piece windscreen and CTIS covers. (Pinikas)

difference between those Humvees in service with the US military and those overseas is little more than the registration number. That said, some overseas variants are often fitted with weapons systems that owe more to past military and political allegiances than the nationality of the suppliers. Bulgaria and Georgia have both fitted their Humvees with Soviet-era PKS general-purpose machine guns. Another former Warsaw Pact nation which operates the Humvee is Poland which has 222 Humvees in use with the 6th Airborne Brigade; a further five are used by Wojska Specjalne (Special Troops Command). The Israeli Army uses some 2,000 Humvees, or Hamer (Hammer), in a range of guises, from border patrol vehicle to the Raccoon surveillance, reconnaissance and image acquisition vehicle. Plasan, an Israeli manufacturer specializing in lightweight armour, have produced armour protection kits for the M1025 and M1100 Armament Carriers. Another licensed producer is the Dirección General de Industria Militar (DGIM) of Mexico. There are differences to the Mexican versions, which are slightly longer, use a Mercedes-Benz diesel engine and have added anti-spall protection in the passenger cabin, as well as protective measures including bulletproof windows. As well as whole vehicle licensing, AM General have provided chassis and components as the base for locally designed vehicles. Swiss manufacturer MOWAG (Motorwagenfabrik AG), utilized the Humvee chassis for the early versions of its Eagle light armoured vehicles. Essentially a reconnaissance platform, the Eagle is in service with Swiss and Danish forces. The Turkish company Otokar Otomotiv ve Savunma Sanayi A.Ş, known simply as Otokar, have also used certain elements of the Humvee in their Cobra armoured tactical vehicle. An interesting variant of the Humvee is

An Azerbaijani Otokar Cobra on parade at Baku.

that made by three Chinese manufacturers, Dongfeng, Shenyang Aircraft Corporation and Xiaolong. All have constructed Humvee clones by importing components and reverse-engineering these with motive powered supplied by a either Steyr or Cummins diesel engines. Only Dongfeng's EQ2050 and Xiaolong's XL2060L Fierce Dragon are in mass production, as both are considerably cheaper than AM General's offerings, and export numbers are slowly increasing.

M998, Echo Company, 2nd Battalion, 9th Marines, Mogadishu International Airport, Operation Restore Hope, May 1992
In late 1992 the Unified Task Force (UNITAF), also known as Operation Restore Hope between May 1992 and December 1993, was set up to help support aid delivers in war-torn Somalia. This M998 Cargo/Troop Carrier was part of Echo Company, 2nd Battalion, 9th Marines who came as part of the Battalion Landing Team (BLT) for the 15th Marine Expeditionary Unit (15th MEU). The 15th were carried on board USS *Tripoli*, USS *Juneau*, and USS *Rushmore*, coming ashore on 9 December 1992. The lack of the standard Marine deep-wading exhaust on the port side of the M998 indicates it kept its wheels dry and came ashore via a Landing Craft Air Cushion (LCAC).

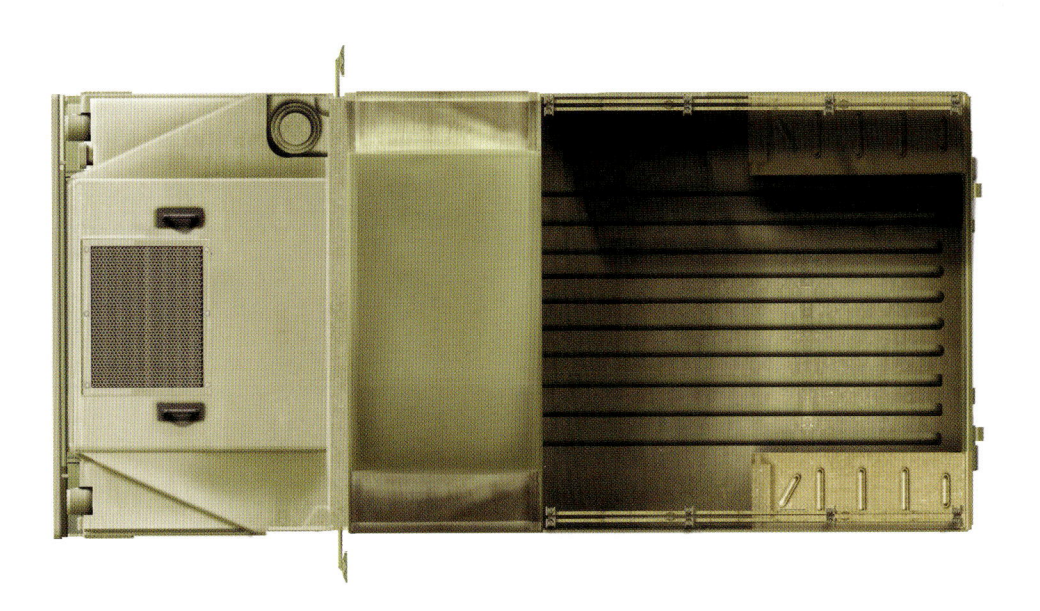

M1025 IFOR, 1st Squadron, 4th US Cavalry, Camp Alicia, Kalesija, Bosnia–Herzegovina, June 1996
This M1025 Armament Carrier was deployed with the US Army's 1st Infantry Division (the Big Red One) where it formed the core of Task Force Eagle in Bosnia-Herzegovina as part of the Implementation Forces (IFOR) in 1996. The key role for some 20,000 US troops deployed in the country as part of IFOR was to uphold the Dayton Peace Accord, protect and help rebuild communities and to provide a visible NATO presence whilst gathering armaments.

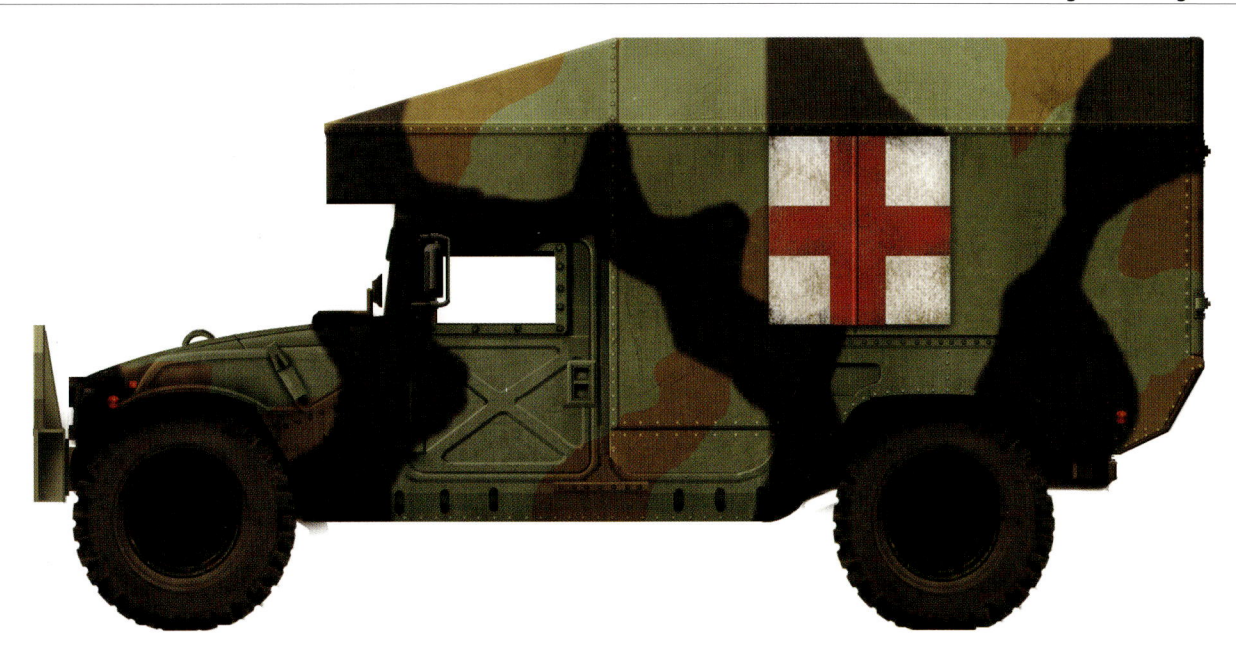

M997A2 Humvee, 407th Ambulance Company, 369th Combat Support Hospital, Puerto Rico, April 2002
This M997 Ambulance belongs to US Army Reserve 407th Ambulance Company (AC), with the 369th Combat Support Hospital (CSH), 65th Regional Support Command (RSC), Puerto Rico, as it would have appeared during the Tradewinds 2002 Field Training Exercise (FTX), on the island of Antigua. The company is often called upon to provide support and healthcare as part of the synchronized Federal emergency response system for immediate assistance after tropical storms.

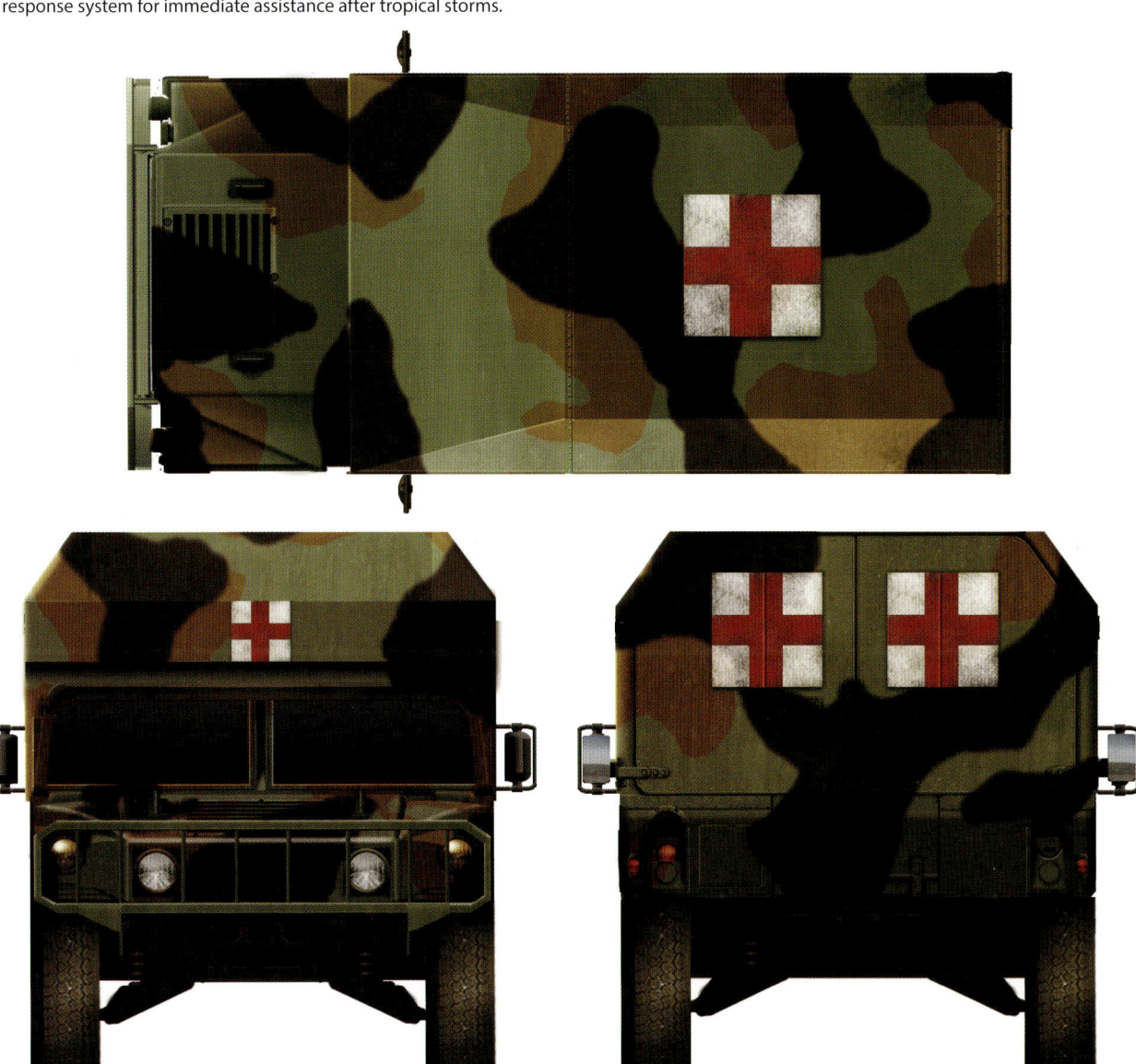

Humvee M1045 TOW, 4th Marine Amphibious Brigade (MAB), Tromso, Norway, March 1987
Between 3 and 29 March 1987 Exercise Cold Winter 1987 took place in the frozen north of Norway, and tested NATO's responses to a possible Soviet incursion. Involving both regular and reserve troops from a host of nations including Norway and Great Britain, the exercise gave the US Marines of the 4th Marine Amphibious Brigade a chance to perfect their cold-weather drills and operational readiness. Under the direction of the Military Airlift Command, the Marines of the 4th MAB, were transported to the exercise by military aircraft.

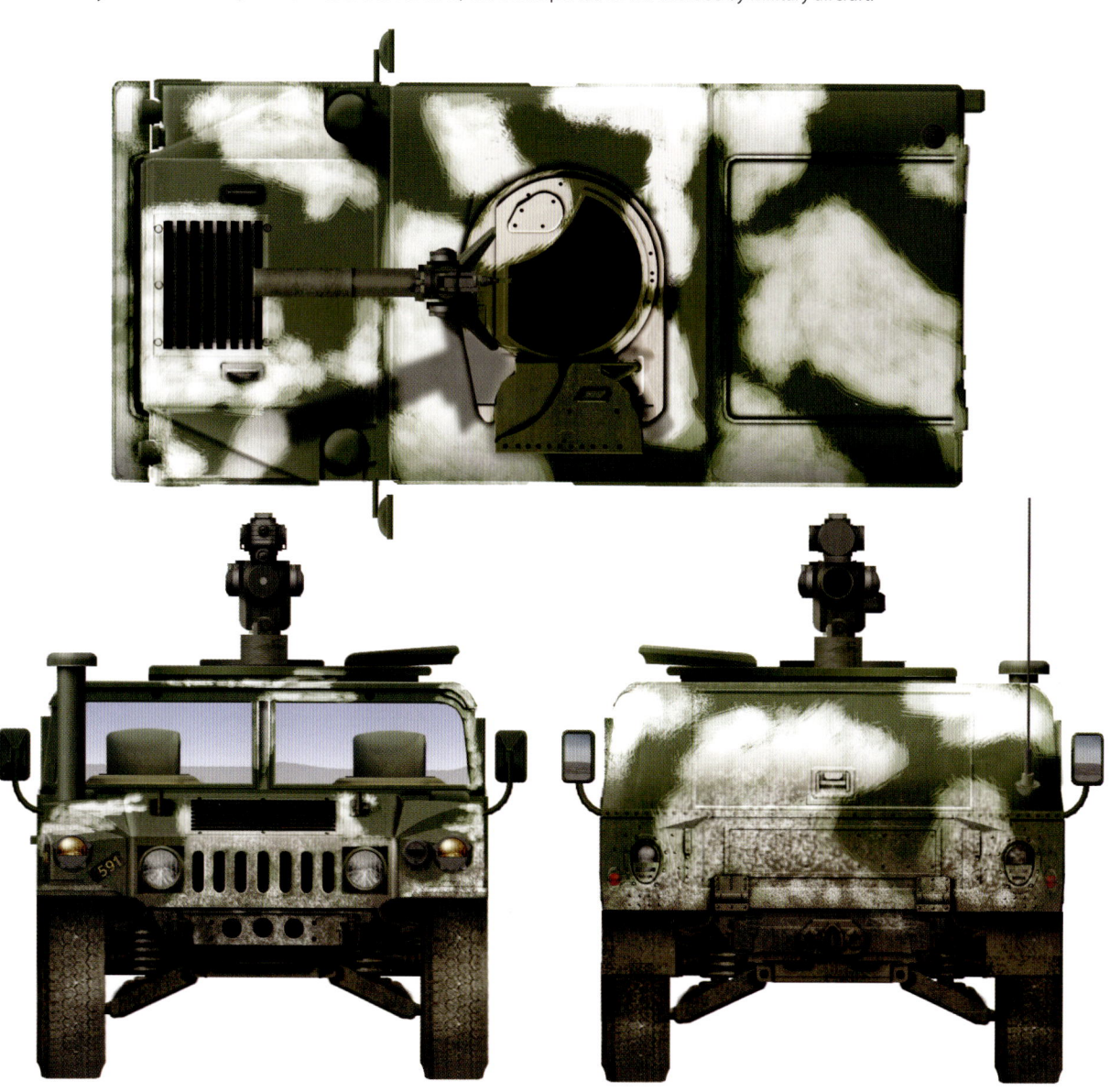

M1025 Armament Carrier, 504th Military Police Battalion (Dragon Fighters), 220th Military Police Brigade, FOB Kalsu, Operation Iraqi Freedom, summer 2004

504th Military Police Battalion worked along the Kuwati–Iraqi border during 2003 where they secured a series of Main Supply Routes (MSRs). This would enable, among other things, the safe coordination and direction of essential troop movements across the border into Iraq. As well as troop movements, the 504th also protected humanitarian aid convoys and the transit of vital infrastructure equipment. During operations the 504th also made more than 70 enemy contacts, capturing more than 200 insurgents and confiscating more than 1,200 weapons. For their efforts the 504th were awarded the Meritorious Unit Commendation (Army) for 2003/4.

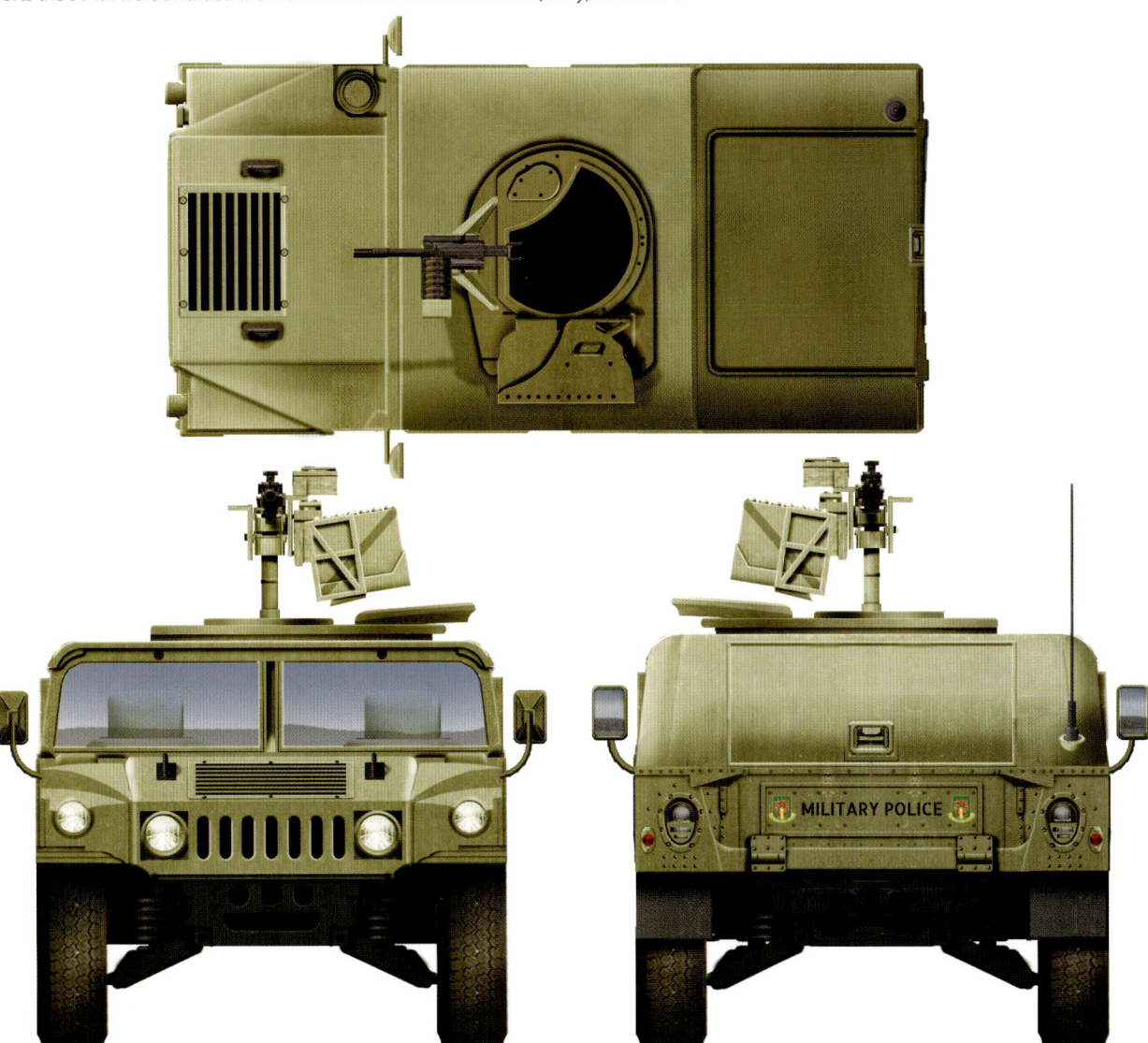

M998 Cargo Carrier, 3rd Battalion, 9th Infantry Regiment, 7th Infantry Division (Light), Palmerola Air Base, Honduras, Operation Golden Pheasant, 1988
Operation Golden Pheasant was an emergency deployment of US troops in Honduras in 1988 to support US-backed Contra forces whose logistical lines in the region were being attacked by Nicaraguan Sandinista government troops. The 7th Infantry Division (Light), who were the Quick Reaction Force (QRF) at the time, deployed elements of the Division to Palmerola Air Base and then onto a military base to secure a local general. Within 72 hours the 7th were supported by the 82nd Airborne Division as well as Marine and Air Force units. The deployment culminated in a live-fire exercise which saw off Sandinista troops back across the border.

ROCMC T75M 20mm Autocannon, 99th Marine Brigade 'Iron Force', Kaohsiung, Republic of China, 2014
The Republic of China Marine Corps (ROCMC) has a well-earned reputation for physical and mental toughness, with battle honours earned in Vietnam and the War on Terror. As befitting their reputation, the ROCMC have fitted some of their crew cab M998s with something a little more powerful than the standard .30 or .50-cal machine gun: the 20mm T75M autocannon. The T75M is a local development of Springfield Armory's 1,500rpm M39 aircraft cannon.

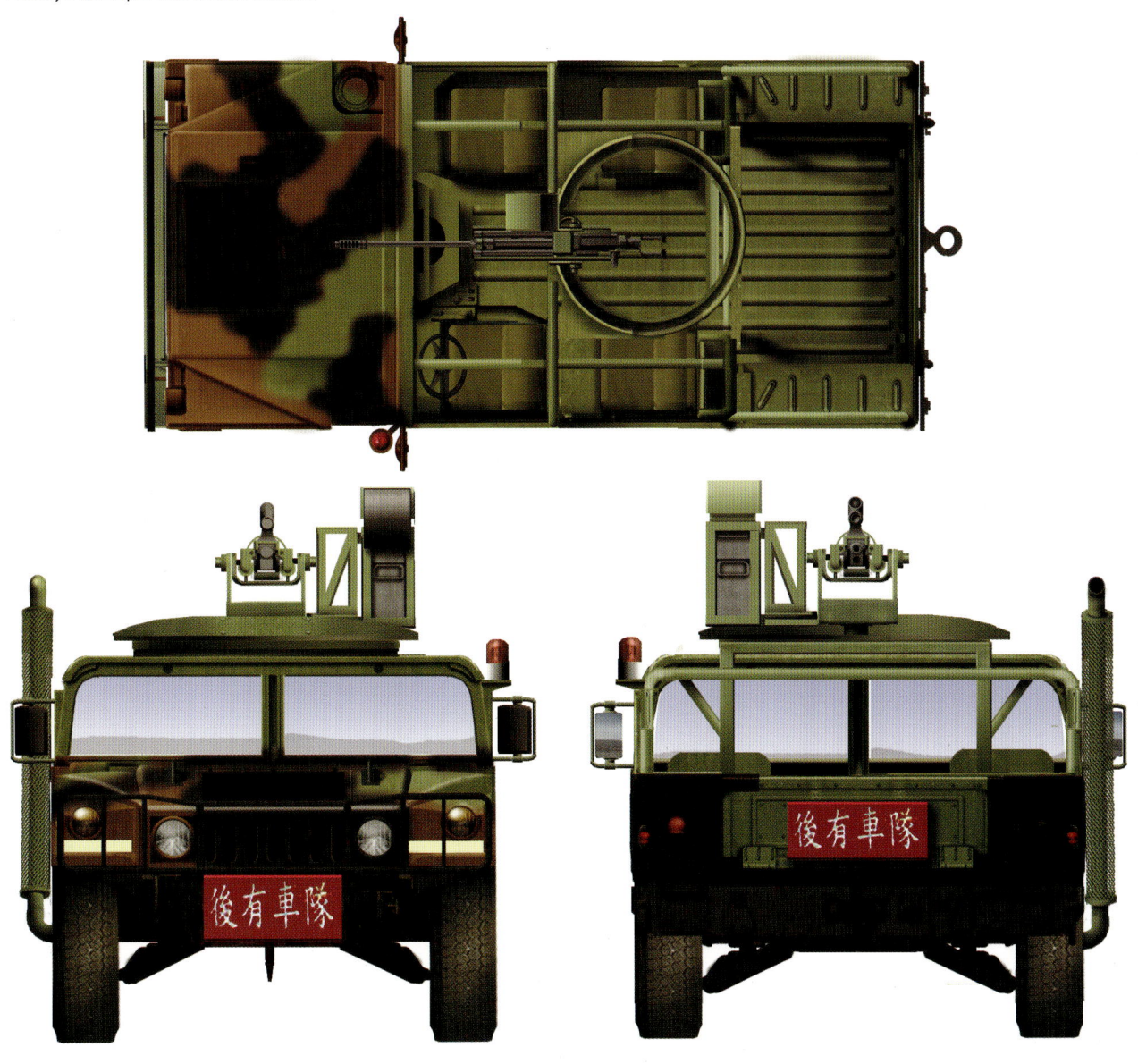

M1025 Special Forces GMV-R, 75th Ranger Regiment, Location: Secret, Date: Undisclosed
The M1025-based Ground Mobility Vehicle (GMV) is a US Special Operations Command (USSOCOM) programme to develop a Humvee purely for strike missions. Using lessons learned from the first Gulf War it has been developed to operate far behind enemy lines. A fully adaptable platform, this GMV-R (Rangers) is able to carry enough stores for up to ten days' mission time, which gives the GMV and its crew the necessary tactical flexibility needed to fulfil their operational task. The design has been used in both the Afghanistan and Iraq theatres with great success.

GMV HUMVEE
Special Forces, Afghanistan, 2000s
1/35 Scale
Jim Wechsler

This model represents a Special Forces Humvee (sometimes nick-named Dumvee) operating in Afghanistan sometime in the mid-2000s. The basic kit is the Tamiya M1025 Humvee. It was modified to the SOF variant using a Legend Production resin and photo-etch conversion set. Further modifications include the IBIS TEK bumper also from Legends, along with metal barrels for the minigun. In addition, the grenade launcher and M240s are built up from Live Resin sets. Additional stowage is from various sources and the ice chest is from DEF models. The ice in the chest is chopped-up clear resin pour blocks with varnish resin poured over them. The figures are a resin set from Blackdog with Leve Resin weapons.

42 HUMVEE

Model Showcase 43

44 HUMVEE

HUMVEE M1114
Afghanistan and Iraq, 2000s
1/35 Scale
Brian Richardson

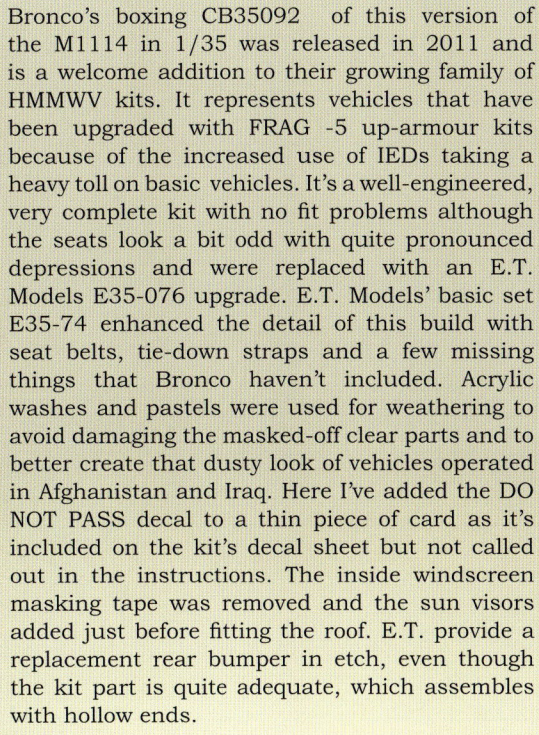

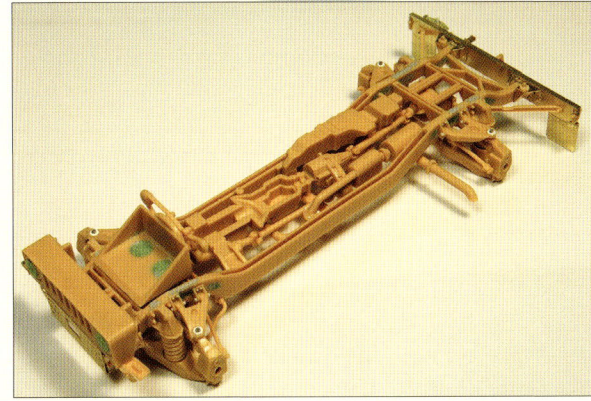

Bronco's boxing CB35092 of this version of the M1114 in 1/35 was released in 2011 and is a welcome addition to their growing family of HMMWV kits. It represents vehicles that have been upgraded with FRAG -5 up-armour kits because of the increased use of IEDs taking a heavy toll on basic vehicles. It's a well-engineered, very complete kit with no fit problems although the seats look a bit odd with quite pronounced depressions and were replaced with an E.T. Models E35-076 upgrade. E.T. Models' basic set E35-74 enhanced the detail of this build with seat belts, tie-down straps and a few missing things that Bronco haven't included. Acrylic washes and pastels were used for weathering to avoid damaging the masked-off clear parts and to better create that dusty look of vehicles operated in Afghanistan and Iraq. Here I've added the DO NOT PASS decal to a thin piece of card as it's included on the kit's decal sheet but not called out in the instructions. The inside windscreen masking tape was removed and the sun visors added just before fitting the roof. E.T. provide a replacement rear bumper in etch, even though the kit part is quite adequate, which assembles with hollow ends.

HUMVEE

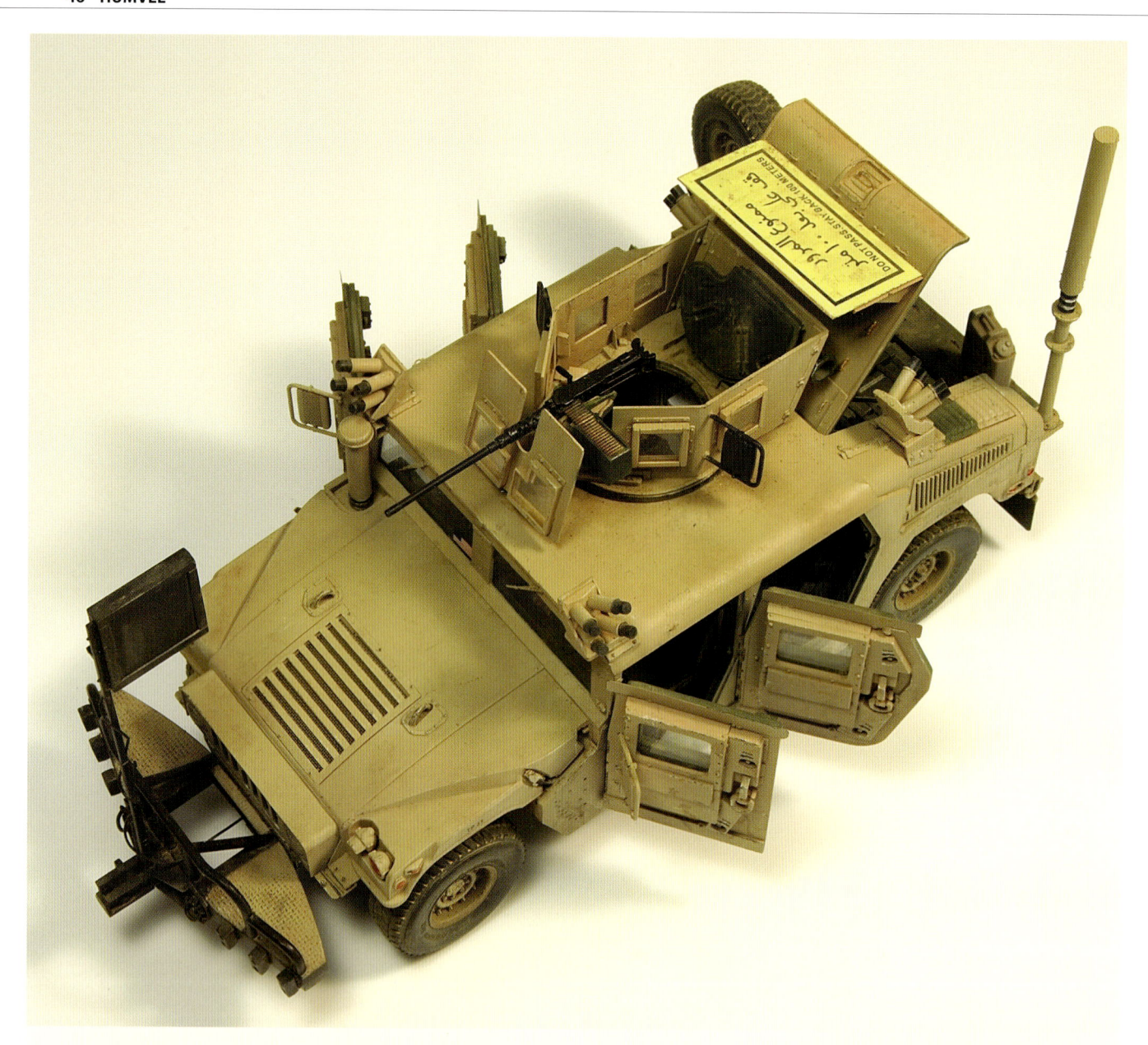

Model Showcase 47

48 HUMVEE

HUMVEE M1025

US UNPROFOR Mission, former Yugoslav Republic of Macedonia (FYROM), Macedonian/Serbian Border, Winter 1993

1/35 Scale
Ben Skipper

This Academy kit is almost 30 years old, and while there are pronounced mould seams, and the vinyl rubber tyres aren't the most accurate, the kit is an extremely straightforward build. Most of the build effort goes into the chassis and cleaning up various seam lines and sink holes left over from the moulding process. The details are crisp and a nice touch is the AM General embossing on the tailgate, highlighting this as an early armament carrier, which well suits the finish. Sadly, the only engine detailing is the bottom portion and gearbox. Once the clean-up was complete, the build was extremely quick, taking a day to complete. Making sure the painting plan was clear in my mind, I decided to finish this Humvee in UN colours as it's a scheme I've never done before and it lends itself to the vehicle. The build was done in three parts: the chassis and lower bodywork, the hard-top bodywork and the doors. This approach let me complete the painting and finish the interior with relative ease. The whole model was primed in matt black before the interior was finished with a coat of Tamiya XF67 NATO Green, with detail painted accordingly. The whole model was then given several light coats of Tamiya XF2 Flat White, which was built up in places, before a varnish with Vallejo acrylic gloss.

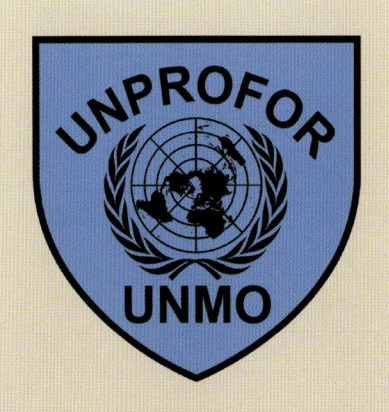

Afterwards the weathering was done using a range of media with attention paid to the plastic vinyl tyres to help mute the surface shine. The UN decals were a mix of spares and Kingfisher Miniatures. As there seemed to be no definitive manner in which the decals were laid down in theatre, I went for the 'it looks right' approach. The vehicle registration marks were modified from decals in the kit, cut with a sharp knife and sealed with varnish to keep them in place. Sadly, the kit didn't come with interior decals, so Eduard placards were used to add colour. The weathering was a mix of paint and ground pastel. I first used a highly diluted mist of Revell Aqua Colour Dark Grey (36378), focusing on the front and the forward sides of the Humvee, before adding a light coat to the trunk. I then applied a light coat of Vallejo Ochre Brown (856) along the sides. For the mud splatters I dipped a flathead brush into the mix and held it alongside the Humvee, blowing air through the bristles from an unloaded airbrush. The effect worked out nicely. The final piece of weathering was to brush ground brown pastel along the lower door edges and on the face of the wheels to add the appearance of fresh mud. Overall, a great kit which is ideal for twentieth-century dioramas and vignettes.

50 HUMVEE

Model Showcase 51

52 HUMVEE

Modelling Products

The Humvee is extremely popular and well served by model manufacturers in all scales over the years. All have their merits with great potential to add multimedia detailing and conversion parts. Kits can also be incorporated into both small vignettes and large-scale dioramas with other genres of model making. As new models are always being produced, this list is purely contemporaneous and features manufacturers that are trading at the time of writing.

Scale Model Kits

The following scale models of the Humvee are currently available to purchase by modellers from their local hobby store. The Humvee has been released in numerous guises over the years and many older models are available on auction websites. All kits are 1/35 unless noted otherwise.

Academy

Academy have been producing kits of the Humvee since 1992, the first version being the M1025, which was quickly followed by the M997 and M998. Pre-2000 kits are presented in boxes with straightforward paintings of the version packaged, akin to the style of Tamiya kits. These original kits were well made, with easy-to-follow instructions and a low part count, helped by the fact that a great many details were moulded into the main body. The tyres were of the vinyl rubber type with any fine tread detail eliminated somewhat by the casting process. That said, they're still a good representation and with considerate weathering will look the part. The decals are minimal, with no interior markings supplied. In terms of moulding there are some unfortunately placed sink marks and some of the seam lines are pretty prolific. However, the seams are easily removed and depending on how you model the Humvee, the sink marks will be mostly be out of sight. A generic gunner figure is also included. By 2011 the original kits were starting to age, and with the introduction of the M1100 series of Humvees, Academy released a new tool kit of the M1151 with correct O-GPK turret. The box art is more dynamic than previous offerings and shows an M1151 driving at speed reacting to an incident of some kind. The kit is spread across eight sand-coloured sprues, and includes a fret of PE and vinyl rubber type, which are split in half. The mouldings are sharp and of better quality than the preceding kits. The parts count is higher, almost double that of the original kits, and includes the FBCB2 computer system and Blue Force Tracking antenna. Other details include two figures, armoured gunner's turret with detailed turret ring and sharper instructions. The M1151 can be completed in three finishes, including the NATO three-tone scheme.

The early box artwork of Academy's M1025 is staid, yet well executed.

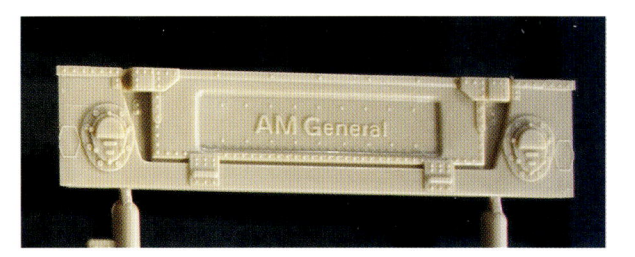

Mouldings are particularly sharp and don't skimp on details.

The vinyl plastic tyre is looking dated, but is still useable, whilst the nylon mesh is supplied for the bonnet radiator louvers.

Bronco

Bronco kits launched their debut Humvee M1114 in 2011, which is available in three versions: CB35136 fitted with the CROWS II remote turret, CB35092 up-armoured HA (heavy) tactical vehicle and CB35080 fitted with a Mk 19 automatic grenade launcher. Presented in beautifully illustrated boxes by the artist Su Lei, these three kits are comprised of up to 15 sprues, cast in dark sand sharply casted plastic, a clear sprue which includes a bottle of water, a fret of PE and a wonderfully crisp decal sheet. A nice touch is the separate packaging for the upper hull and wheel tread elements.

Bronco spoil the modeller with these kits, including such details as the fans for the air-conditioning unit, engine detailing and split-moulded gunner's hatch.

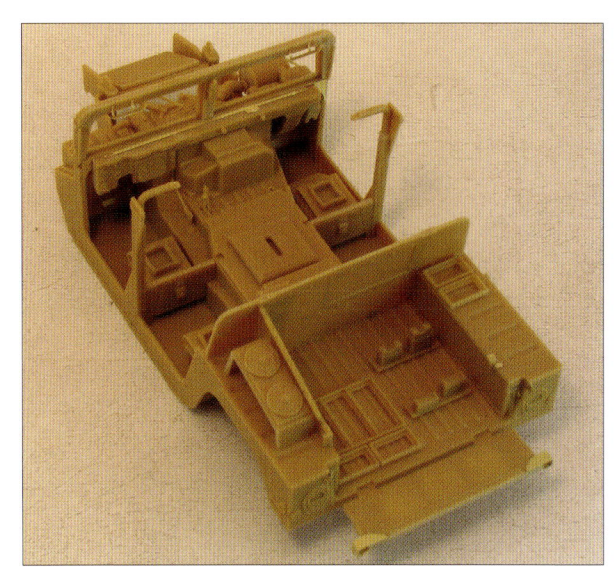

Bronco's M1114 Humvee interior. (Jim Wechsler)

Bronco's M1114 Humvee chassis. (Jim Wechsler)

Su Lei's artwork is exceptionally sharp, and takes a different angle when depicting the subject model, focusing on the blunt nose of the Humvee, giving it a more aggressive look.

The real party piece of these kits is the three-part wheels featuring a tread and sides; however, the sharp-eyed will notice a unique spelling error in the company name, GOOD YEAP, made, perhaps, to get round licensing issues. Decals are crisp with a focus on Iraq and Afghan operations and the instructions are exceptionally clear and include a colour painting chart, which when followed will produce some handsome models. Bronco has also produced a plastic kit of the CROWS II remote-controlled gun mount for their M1100 series models. Bronco kits have a fair reputation for their high quality, but it comes at a cost. So, if you're tackling these as a novice builder, especially the photo etch, do take your time.

Italeri
Italeri's Humvee kit has been around probably the longest of all manufacturers. It was first released as the M1025 in 1987; since then, the range has grown to include the five original versions of the Humvee as well as the Avenger anti-aircraft system. The age of the kits is starting to show, and there are some awkward sink marks in the moulding process to overcome, though some are well hidden by the building process. The decals are minimal, with no interior markings supplied. The boxes, with art by Giuseppe Rava, include wonderfully clear colour painting guides on the sides and rear face.

As one would expect from Italeri, the kits are the product of sound research and the building is relatively straightforward via clear instructions. These Italeri kits are well worth seeking out and as Italeri do tend to do re-releases, finding one is never difficult. Italeri Humvees have also been re-boxed and sold by Revell, Tamiya, Testors and Zvezda in the past.

Giuseppe Rava's box art as always makes any Italeri kit stand out and the M998 is no exception.

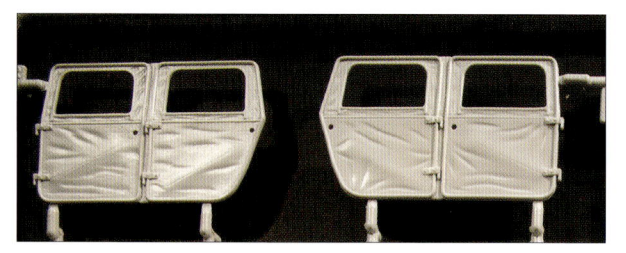

The detailing of the fabric doors is as crisp as it is elegant.

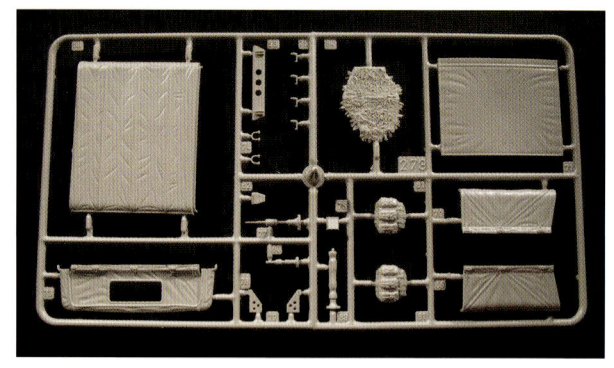

Sprues are well laid out and the overhead tilt echoes the details of the doors. Note the camouflage netting.

Hobby Den
Irish 1/72 resin masters Hobby Den have produced a series of simple Humvee kits. These wonderfully sculpted kits include the TOW Carrier (HD82), M1025 (HD83), .50 cal (HD84), Avenger, M1035 Ambulance (HD2), M1042 Shelter Carrier (HD29) and the Objective Gunner Protection Kit (O-GPK) Turret (HD118). The kits are pretty straightforward and would sit nicely in a vignette or diorama with an aircraft or two.

The shelter carrier is a cracking little resin kit, ready to deploy to a fine scale diorama.

Model Miniature

Model Miniature have produced two 1/72 kits of Humvees in Israeli service: the Hamer Racoon reconnaissance vehicle (MM-R070) and the Hamer Lynx communications relay system (MM-R096) and a set of corresponding wheels (MM-R091). The kits are supplied with beautifully sculpted Israeli Defense Forces (IDF) figures and come complete with photo-style assembly instructions.

Model Miniature have also made two sets of the decals for the Israeli Memugan Hamer, in 1/72 (MM-D001) and 1/35 (MM-D002). These sets provide enough registration marks for three different vehicles, though interior decals aren't provided. Printing is crisp and the instructions are clear with photographs of a real Hamer used to illustrate decal locations.

Hamer Lynx communications vehicle and figure: nicely moulded with some great detail.

MR Modellbau

MR Modellbau are renowned for their excellent small-scale 1/87 resin kits and with the Humvee they have produced three different sets of resin models, with each set including two vehicles. The vehicles are examples of the M998 and M1038 pickup types and feature these with two differing shelters (MR87120), the S-788 and S-1497-type shelters (MR87121), and M997 Ambulance (MR87139). The ambulance body is available as a separate conversion kit (MR87083), set MR-87118 includes two M998 'Helmet' hard tops, MR-87119 supplying two workshop backs and MR-87126 the soft top for the M1035A2 Ambulance.

Set MR-87145 is an early Iraq War update set for Dragon's 1/72 M1025-based models featuring the FS3 fire-support sensor. Currently Dragon aren't producing 1/72 Humvees, but the kits occasionally come up on auction sites and are highly sought after due to their fine details and easy build nature.

MR Modellbau have also produced rear bumper updates for M998A2/M1025A2 (MR-35411). The set also includes inner and outer struts, support blocks for the shelter carrier version along with stiffening brackets, retaining rings and U-shackles. The set is designed for Tamiya kits, but can be adapted for use with other manufacturers' kits.

Tamiya

Given Tamiya's often quick response to new military hardware, they were somewhat reticent in developing their own version of the Humvee, relying on Italeri's mouldings until 2003. Their first kit, 35263, was the M1025 which allowed the modeller to build either the Mk 19 automatic grenade launcher or .50-cal versions. The kit comes with two figures, four finishing options, including desert, and depicts the early-type M1025 as well as options for a USMC version. Moulded in sand-colour plastic, the kit is complete with two differing bonnet louvres, the earlier type featuring fewer bars compared to later M1100 series types. Early and A1 updates wing mirrors are also included.

Mouldings are sharp and are spread across six sprues including clear plastic. The tyres are of the rubber vinyl type, but like the Academy wheels, these are easily upgraded with any number of resin offerings. The second kit is the M1046 TOW Carrier, 35627, with winch, CIP and extra armour. This kit features all the key elements of the M1025 kit but includes a host of extra detail necessary for the TOW version, including the dismounted tripod mount. Again, the modeller is able to finish the kit in four differing versions, including USMC.

As well as the 1/35 models, Tamiya have added the Humvee to their burgeoning 1/48 range. First launched in 2009 (32563) as the pickup cargo type M998, two M1025 versions soon followed: 32567 was fitted with the Mk 19 grenade launcher and 89790 with the .50 cal. All three are comparable in finish quality to their larger 1/35 counterparts, and include the now ubiquitous vinyl rubber tyres. All kits come with Tamiya's easy-to-read instructions and decals, which include interior markings, even for the 1/48 kits.

All kits are presented in wonderfully illustrated boxes with the 1/48 kit being treated to a full action scene with a squadron of M1 Abrams and supported by AH-64 Apaches.

M1025 exterior.

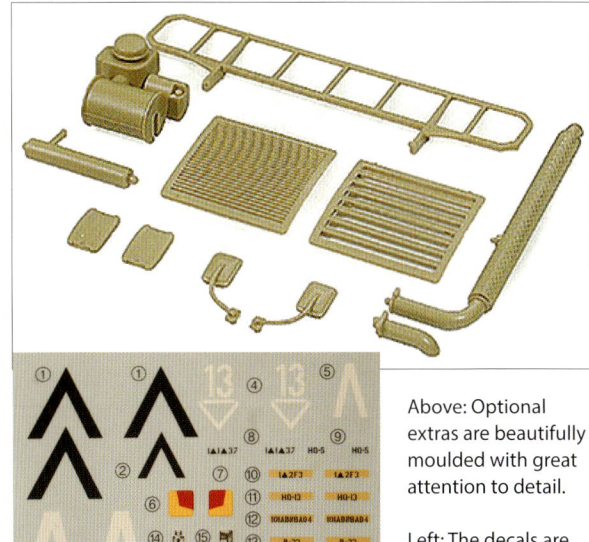

Above: Optional extras are beautifully moulded with great attention to detail.

Left: The decals are wonderfully sharp and include basic interior decals.

The TOW carrier interior is wonderfully complete, even down to the dismounted tripod mount.

The 1/48 box shows the gallant Humvee leading the charge across the desert, a fun depiction of a great little kit

PE and Resin Detailing

There is an abundance of detailing for the Humvees with manufacturers offering the modeller items in resin, photo etch and 3D printing. Unless noted otherwise, all decals are in 1/35.

Mixed Media Detailing

Black Dog

Black Dog offer seven conversion and upgrade kits include the Special Forces GMV (T35076) which is also available as a set with a resin and PE Light Medium Tactical Vehicle (LMTV) (T35078). Also available is the Danish Special Forces Jülkat (T35213) and the unique snow truck (T35215). As Tamiya's kits lack a detailed engine bay, Black Dog have produced an exceptionally well-detailed yet simply constructed three-part engine and radiator set (T35210).

For the 1/48 modeller there is an excellent and beautifully appointed Iraq War M1025 accessory set (T48034), and for IDF modellers a wonderful multimedia upgrade (T48058). This includes new top, doors and weapons station (T48058). The final kit is a front portion of a destroyed Humvee, designed specifically as a vignette base for the modeller that wants to portray something a little more dramatic (D35018).

Black Dog's GMV kit is filled with detail and is a vignette in itself.

Left: The 1/48 Iraq M1025 upgrade kit for Tamiya's M1025 is as detailed as their 1/35 resin upgrades.

Centre left: The 1/48 IDF M1025 Tamiya upgrade features the Hamer's unique slab-sided upper body.

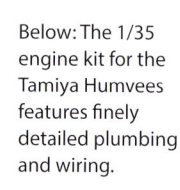

Below: The 1/35 engine kit for the Tamiya Humvees features finely detailed plumbing and wiring.

D-Toys/Division Miniature

D-Toys/Division Miniature are a Korean company who have produced no less than four replacement wheel sets for the Humvee in both 1/48 and 1/35. The 1/48 set (DT48001) features mid-life tyres under load and is intended for Tamiya kits. Set DT35015 features mid-life tyres and rims and is for Tamiya kits only. DT35037 and DT35038 feature later-life tyres and rims and are suitable for use with Academy, Bronco and Tamiya kits and all feature tyres under load. Beautifully cast with excellent attention to detail, this would make a model of the M1100 series stand out.

Modelling Products

ET Model
ET Model have seen their range of PE and resin kits grow over the past few years. Building a reputation for well-engineered and challenging kits, ET Model have certainly stepped up with their offerings for the Humvee. They've produced two tyre sets, ER35-015, which are weight-bearing tyres, and ER35-016, which are the all-terrain wheels; both feature mid-life tyres and rims.

The first of the PE kits, EA35-050, is a set of Combat Identification Panels (CIPs) that were used to great effect in Iraq and Afghanistan. Kits EA35-074 to EA35-078 are designed for Bronco's M1114 Humvee and these really make the detail pop. From the Gunner Protection Kit (EA35-075) to the Blue Force Tracker & SINCGAR Unit (EA35-078) these multimedia kits give the modeller an opportunity to produce an awe-inspiring fine-scale model of the Humvee.

Legend
The multimedia experts at Legend have really gone all out on the Humvee, producing an awe-inspiring and beautifully executed range of detailing kits for the Humvee. LF1227 is intended for use with Academy's M1114 and features, among many other things, a PE gunner's turret. LF1218 is a basic multimedia upgrade set featuring smoke-grenade dischargers and the rear flank air-conditioning ventilation grille. LF1212 is a GMV conversion set for Tamiya and Academy kits and features a host of extras, including mid-life tyres and rims, as well as numerous mission-ready stores. Set LF1207 is a Frag 5 conversion set for the Tamiya kit, featuring updated doors, full interior details and a rear-mounted spare wheel on a swing mount.

LF1206 is a Rhino anti-IED device that is mounted on the front of the Humvee. The Rhino is a Passive Infrared Defeat System that uses heat to detonate hidden IEDs. LF1203 is an armour update kit for early armament carriers in the Iraq and Afghan theatres, whilst LF1195 is a simple front bust guard upgrade to the IBIS Tek bumper, which is designed to nudge obstacles out of the vehicle's path. Another interesting projection conversion is the SPARK (Self-Protection Adaptive Roller Kit) mine roller, LF1246, pushed in front of the Humvee to detonate mines and IEDs buried beneath the road surface.

Sets LF1192 and LF1196 are multimedia Gunner Protection Kits for early and later M1100 series Humvees; set LF1192 is worthy of consideration, if only for its accuracy. LF1193 and LF1194 are M1151 conversions kits for Tamiya kits. LF3D007 is a resin-sculpted TOW turret and M60 mount that can be fitted to the armament carrier version of the Humvee. All are beautifully observed and feature an entirely reworked superstructure and interior.

For the IDF modeller set LF1159 is an excellent rendition of the standard armament carrier and features the correct superstructure whilst LF1145 is a full conversion kit for the open-topped TOW carrier. Legend have also produced a conversion kit for Academy's M997 Ambulance, which, together with the other sets, gives the IDF modeller a huge range of options.

The M1114 detailing kits are some of the finest PE a modeller will encounter. Note the mid-life resin wheels and M2 body.

All bells and whistles on this fully fitted-out M1114. Of note is the PE gunner's turret.

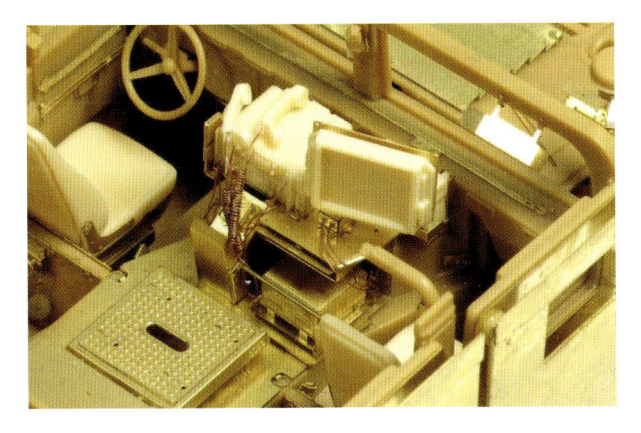

The comms setup upgrade is stunning. The handset spiral wire is achieved by wrapping fine wire around a sewing needle.

LF12A6 Rhino is well detailed and a great multimedia kit.

58 HUMVEE

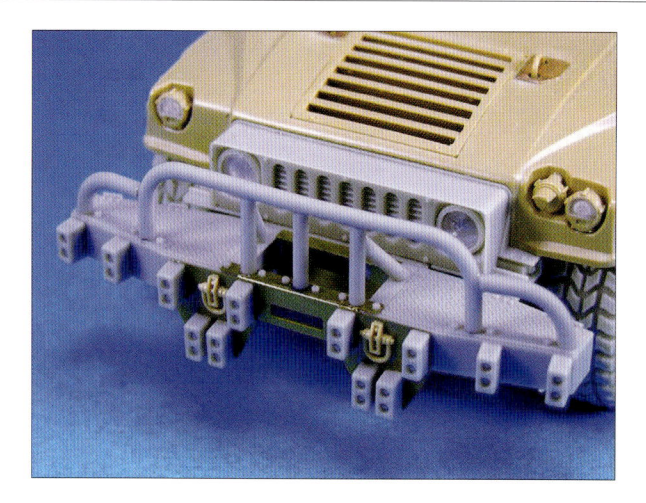

LF1195 IBIS: the interesting bumper would make a great addition to any kit headed for a diorama.

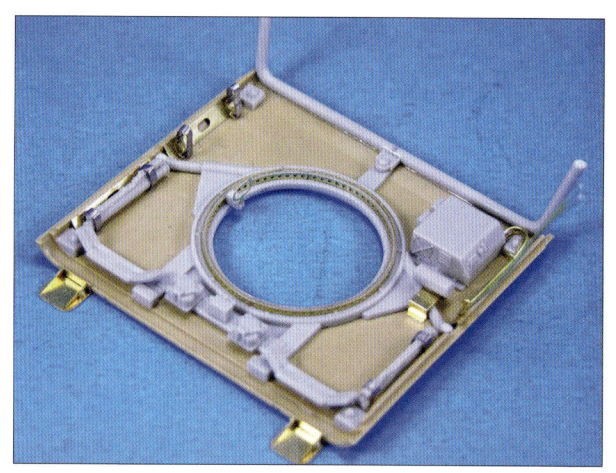

LF1212 GMV roof detail shows that Legend really have thought of everything.

Resin TOW gunner station kit is a great update and beautifully moulded.

LF1246 SPARK mine roller is a wonderful little kit that shows how adaptable the Humvee really is.

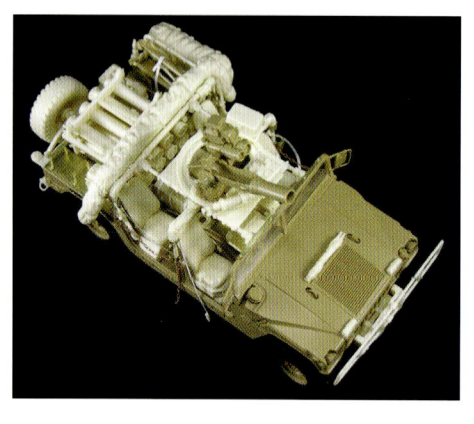

LF1145 IDF TOW is a great conversion kit for the IDF enthusiast.

Finally, Legend have produced a stowage set, LF1114, to enable the modeller to festoon their creations with all manner of personal and mission-essential kit.

Perfect Scale Modellbau

German Perfect Scale Modellbau have produced a USMC conversion kit for the Bronco M11144 featuring new doors, as well as the prominent mast-mounted dome of the Chameleon. Chameleon is a tactical signal emulator system which is designed to mimic both military and civilian radio frequencies to trigger mobile phone-activated IEDs. The resin is sharp and the PE details are beautifully arranged, especially the door furniture. This kit is clearly for the experienced modeller as some of the PE elements are complex, but with patience will reward the modeller immensely.

Just shows how much detail multimedia kits can provide the modeller with.

Modelling Products 59

S&S Models
S&S Models have produced two interesting kits for the Humvee in 1/72 scale for the small-scale modeller, a wonderfully accurate GMV kit produced in white metal and resin, and a white metal GPK turret, which will fit any armament carrier kit thanks to a specially designed conversion mount.

SOL Model
SOL Model has produced a resin engine and replacement bonnet, with PE debris guard, for Bronco's M1114. The detailing is exceptional and the kits relatively easy to assemble due to its low parts count.

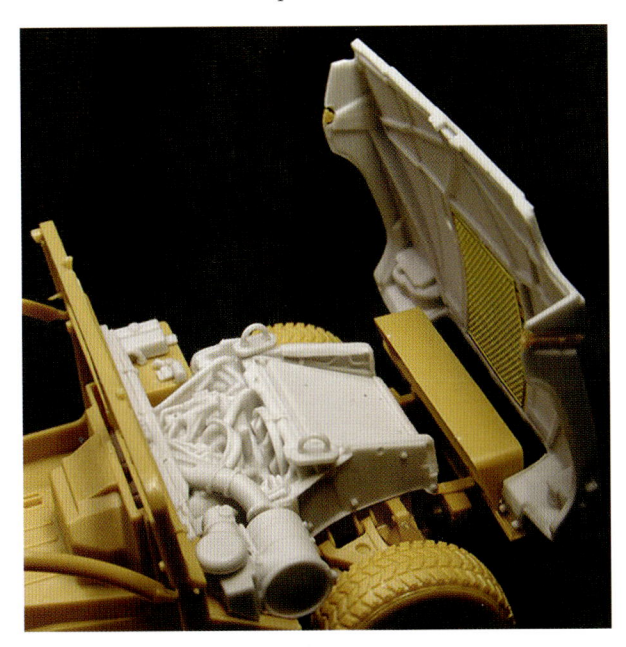

The SOL engine is a model in itself, the replacement bonnet features correct strengthening to add to the realism.

Voyager Model
Voyager Model are a prolific detailing producer and the Humvee has not escaped their attention. The multimedia kits are always well researched and a delight to work with. It is worth noting that many of these kits are often made available as separate units, such as PEA232 USMC M1114 spaced amour and PEA2461/35 bulletproof doors.

For those keen on modelling USMC Humvees, set PE35397 converts the Bronco M1114 accordingly and features a full interior as well as CIP and smoke dischargers. Set PE354011 is based on a Frag 5 armoured Humvee and features a host of PE detailing as well as a Rhino counter-IED. PE35422 is another USMC conversion for the M1151 version, designed for the Academy kits, featuring improved door details and features the Objective Gunner Protection Kit with roof.

Set PEA1191 is a generic PE detailing kit featuring CIP with door handle inserts, radio mounts and USMC exhaust shrouds. Resin road wheels, set PEA231, slightly weighted, are supplied in a mid-life pattern and spare. Voyager have also made a Super Swamper all-terrain tyres set, PEA2451, which, again, is wonderfully cast and features mid-life rim furniture. Following the resin upgrade theme, set PEA234 is a replacement resin high back seat set for USMC vehicles. PEA236 is a turret kit for the armament carrier and features an accurately sculpted Mk 19 grenade launcher.

For communications there are three sets: PEA254 features the Warlock ECM antenna, PEA260 a telescopically mounted Warlock ECM antenna and PEA259 the Blue Force Tracker and SINCGAR unit. Each is beautifully made and the moulding of the Blue Force Tracker and SINCGAR hardware is impressive,

The full M1151 upgrade kit is as impressive as it is complete.

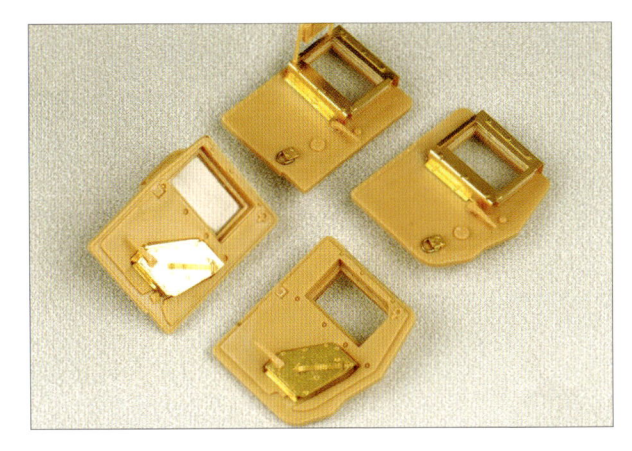

The door detailing, including the D-ring rescue pulls, is well designed.

IED countermeasures galore.

worthy of mounting in any Iraq- or Afghanistan-deployed Humvee.

Photo Etch Detailing

Hauler

Czech concern Hauler has produced a range of four PE sets to help upgrade Tamiya's 1/48 M998, M1038 and M1025 early Humvees. Set HLX48270 is a basic exterior detailing kit for the M1025, which, with companion interior detail kit HLX48271, gives the Tamiya Humvee that little something extra to help bring the kit alive. Kit HLX48298 provides interior and exterior detailing for the basic M988/M1038 Cargo Carrier version of the Humvee. Hauler also produce a set of mid-life tyres and rims for the Humvee, HLX48301, which are wonderfully cast and detailed and are an improvement on the original kit's rubber tyres.

It's the little things that impress; in this case the cutouts on the CIP panel stand out.

This updated comms set is something else; the keyboard is a wonderful touch.

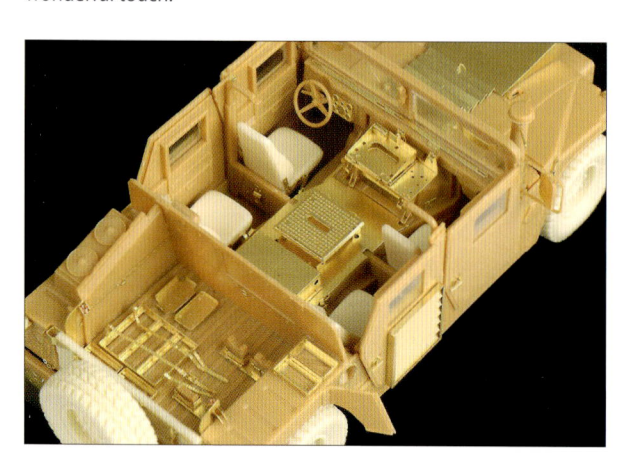

The resin seats with their PE details are a nice touch.

M998 cargo and troop carrier detailing set.

M1025 detailing set; note the M60 ammo belt.

Hauler#4 Mid-life tyre set.

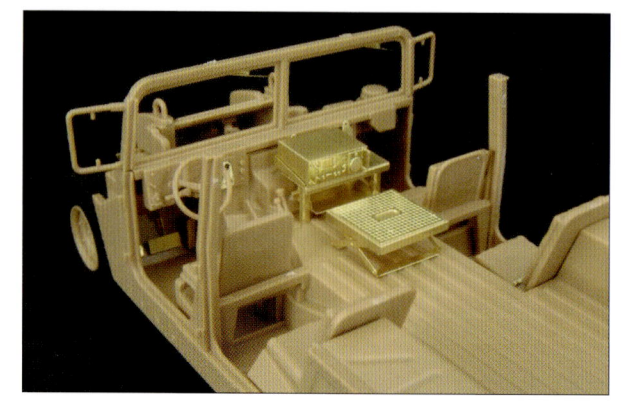

Interior details for all Humvees.

Flyhawk Model

Flyhawk Model have produced two PE detailing sets for Dragon's 1/72-scale Humvee 7296 and 7297. Set FH72013 is for the M1046 TOW Carrier and features CIP panels, rear-view mirror mounts, bonnet grille and brush guard, whilst set FH72013 is for the M998 and features the same elements as the M1046 kit as well as checkerboard flooring for the cargo bay and a shield for the mounted M60. Both kits are straightforward enough and add simple, yet eye-catching details.

FlyHawk M1046 shows PE detail in 1/72 and can be as strong as 1/35 offerings

Resin and 3D Kits and Detailing

Blast Models

Blast Models from France have produced an amazing range of precisely sculpted resin add-ons for the later M1100 series Humvees in the Iraq and Afghan theatres. As well as wheels and rims (BL35162K), Blast have also produced a full range of IED countermeasures including the SPARK roller (BL35150K) and Warlock (BL35160K). There is also an armoured door upgrade (BL35052K) and CROWS remote-controlled gun mount.

Def Model

Def Model are synonymous with quality resin casts and for the Humvee modeller they deliver the goods and have produced no less than three tyre sets: DW35002A for Academy's M1151, DW35003A mid-life type for Academy and Tamiya kits and DW35004A early type for Tamiya M998 and M1025. They also produce two tyre sets for 1/48 Tamiya kits, DW48002 mid-life type and DW48003 early type. All sets are sculpted to show the tyres in weighted mode and include painting masks.

FC Model Trend

FC Model Trend have produced a resin and 3D-printed spare wheel and bumper-mounted carrier for Tamiya's M1025 model (35582). This is intended for use with IDF or Portuguese Humvees. The detailing of the replacement bumper and spare wheel mount is crisp with an early tyre being supplied.

Hobby Fan

AFV Club's in-house resin concern Hobby Fan have produced an ROC Marine Corps T75 20mm cannon conversion kit for the Academy Humvee. As with all Hobby Fan resin kits, this kit is well sculpted and a must for ROC enthusiasts.

ROC Marine Corps T75 20mm cannon resin and PE conversion kit.

Modell Trans Modellbau

Modell Trans Modellbau have produced two 1/72 shelters which would make great additions to a diorama Humvee. MTD7239 is the S788 lightweight multipurpose shelter and MTD7239 is the smaller S250 shelter. Both are beautifully modelled single-piece castings.

Panzer Art

Panzer Art have produced two resin kits for the Humvee: early-type wheels (RE35-075) and Humvee with sandbag armour (RE35-310). The wheel set features early rims and includes a spare; the castings are of the usual high standard, but be aware that the wheel profile is cast as fully inflated without weight bulges. The sandbag protection set is an interesting choice and intended for the armament carrier types.

This sandbag protection is, if anything, a very interesting conversion of the Humvee.

Priamide Models

Priamide Models have produced over 20 3D-printed detailing kits for the M1100 series Humvees and GMVs. Sets include pioneer tools, up-armour kits and M1151 to M1165 conversion kits. The kits are produced in clear plastic and have been designed around Tamiya's M1025 kit. Well researched, well designed and well printed, the parts are attached to a traditional-style sprue-type structure.

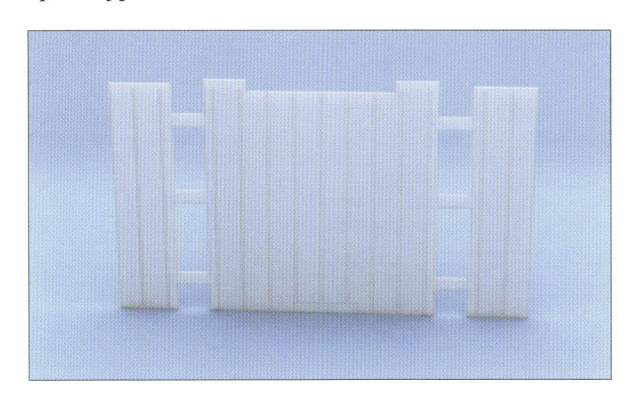

GMV cargo bay armour plating.

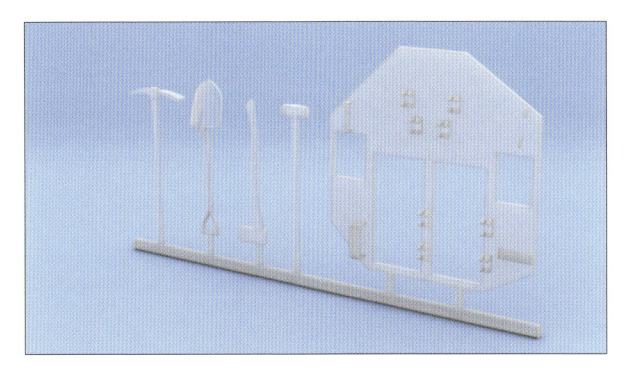

GMV pioneer tools with bonnet-mounted tool housing.

Tank Workshop

Tank Workshop have produced two sets of early Humvee tyres and wheels. Set TWS 350090 features a straightforward tyre whilst the brilliantly imaginative set TWS 350089 features tyres with snow chains. An interesting feature to these sets is that the casts have hollow hub centres which means they can be mounted on any 1/35 model of the Humvee.

Snow-chained tyres are a rarity, so these early Humvee types are most welcome.

Decals

All decals in this section have been specifically designed for use with the Humvee Family of Vehicles, covering the type from conception to present. Unless noted otherwise all decals are in 1/35.

Archer

US manufacturer Archer have built a great reputation for giving the modeller high-quality detailed decals that make vehicle interiors stand out (AR35282). The print quality is exceptional and extra decals are included just in case of any mishaps, or if the modeller is finishing a couple of models. Colours are in register and true shades have been used for the blacks as opposed to variants of grey. Whilst on larger decals this would look too toylike, given the use for smaller areas such as dials and notices, the black brings out the white details nicely.

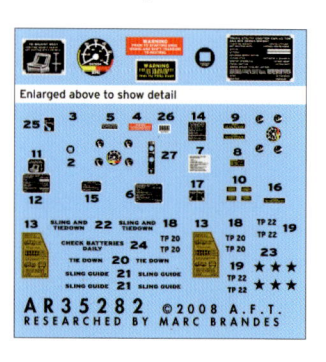

These Humvee decals are a great asset especially for those wanting to model the Humvee in its GMV or stripped-down configurations.

Eduard

Eduard have produced a sheet of colour etch placards for the Humvee (TP516). Designed for the interior, these PE-based placards are well made and researched and while intended for Tamiya's M1025 kit, they'll suit any member of the Humvee family. These placards are well researched, with the colours standing out nicely without being too brash. As a bonus there are enough placards to furnish a couple of models. As always with Eduard, the instructions are well designed and concise.

Echelon Fine Decals

Echelon Fine Decals have produced six sets of decals for Humvees, including the Special Forces GMV (D356253), in US service in Afghanistan and Iraq. The sets include a generic ISAF markings set for the M1151 (D356015). The next set (D356182) is for the M1151s used by the 101st Airborne in Iraq. Featuring the markings of the 327th, 187th and 506th Regiments, these decals are well researched and beautifully rendered. Set D356209 is for early-Iraq M1025s, M1046s and M1114s and features markings for seven separate vehicles. D356233 is an interesting set as it provides markings for the M1117 and M1078 in Iraq and the 11th Armoured Cavalry at the Fort Irwin National Training Center. The real treat for the modeller is set T35022, which covers the Iraq and Afghan conflict Humvees in both American and Iraqi service. As well as featuring markings for 14 versions, the set features generic markings including tyre pressures and flammable liquid markings. This set comes with a booklet awash with photographs for reference. Whilst initially appearing to be visually busy, it's a great way to show off markings in theatre. As always, the rendering of decals is sharp, true to form and the colour palette, especially the yellows, is on point and won't disappoint.

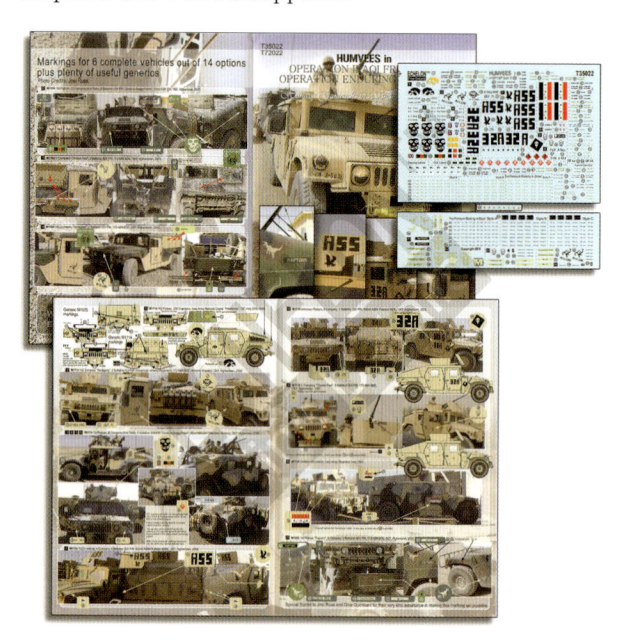

Pack T35022 is the last word in detailing. No less than 14 different vehicles can be detailed with this pack.

ToRo Model

Tomasz Mańkowski of ToRo Model has been producing decals for Humvees in Polish military service for over 20 years. His Humvee set (35D04) provides the modeller with marking for six distinct Polish Humvees and the opportunity to produce several more though blank numberplates and additional numbers. Also included are International Security Assistance Force (ISAF) markings and Arabic translations identifying the Humvees as Polish. Decals are for the M998, M1025 and M1100 series of Humvees. Afghan decals are also available in set 35D50, *Polish Army Vehicles on Foreign Missions*. Instructions are clear and the decals are stunningly sharp, with no overflow of the white and red national markings. The same decal set is also available in 1/48 (48D04) and 1/72 (72D04). ToRo Models have also produced a simple PE and clear plastic front gunner shield for the Humvee (35021).

Modeller Jim Wechsler shows what can be done with a good kit and some carefully selected aftermarket products, as well as scratch building and a lot of patience. This model represents an M1114 Humvee with mine rollers serving in Iraq in the mid-2000s with an Explosive Ordnance Unit (EOD). It shows the vehicle parked on a road with one soldier in protective gear, a second preparing the Talon EOD robot for deployment and the third sitting in the Humvee at the CROWS weapon station to provide cover. The basic kit is the 1/35 scale Bronco M1114 Humvee. It has been upgraded with the CROWS remote weapon station from Blast Models with a metal barrel from RB Models, the IBIS Tek bumper from Legend Productions, a SPARK Mine Roller also from Blast Models and ECM jammers from Legend and Voyager. The figures are from Black Dog and Legend and the stowage from multiple sources. In addition, the Talon Robot is from AFV Club. Electrical wires are made from solder wire and the straps are mostly lead foil strips.

64 HUMVEE